Enterprise

JAVABEANS™

by Example

GW00601182

Enterprise

JAVABEANS™

by Example

Henri Jubin · Jürgen Friedrichs
and the Jalapeño Team

IBM International Technical Support Organization
Austin, Texas 78758

Prentice Hall PTR
Upper Saddle River, New Jersey 07458
http://www.phptr.com

Library of Congress Cataloging-in-Publication Data

Jubin, Henri.
    Enterprise JavaBeans by example / Henri Jubin, Jürgen Friedrichs,
    and the Jalapeño Team.
        p.   cm.
        ISBN 0-13-022475-8 (alk. paper)
        1. Java (Computer program language) 2. JavaBeans.
    I. Friedrichs, Jürgen. II. Jalapeño Team. III. Title.
    QA76.73.J38J82   1999
    005.2'762--dc21

99-28557
CIP

Editorial/production supervision: *Jane Bonnell*
Cover design director: *Jayne Conte*
Cover design: *Bruce Kenselaar*
Cover illustration: *Karen Strelecki*
Copyeditor: *Mary Lou Nohr*

Manufacturing manager: *Pat Brown*
Acquisitions editor: *Michael Meehan*
Editorial assistant: *Bart Blanken*
Marketing manager: *Bryan Gambrel*

© 2000 by International Business Machines Corporation

Published by Prentice Hall PTR
Prentice-Hall, Inc.
Upper Saddle River, New Jersey 07458

Prentice Hall books are widely used by corporations and government agencies for training, marketing, and resale.
The publisher offers discounts on this book when ordered in bulk quantities. For more information, contact
Corporate Sales Department, Phone: 800-382-3419; FAX: 201-236-7141;
E-mail: corpsales@prenhall.com
Or write: Prentice Hall PTR, Corporate Sales Dept., One Lake Street, Upper Saddle River, NJ 07458.

Disclaimer: The information contained in this book has not been submitted to any formal IBM test and is distributed as is. The information about non-IBM products in this book has been supplied by the vendor and IBM assumes no responsibility for its accuracy or completeness. The use of this information or the implementation of any of these techniques is the reader's responsibility and depends on the reader's ability to evaluate and integrate them into his or her operational environment.

AIX, AS/400, CICS, DB2, IBM, OS/2, OS/390, S/390, VisualAge, and WebSphere Application Server are trademarks or registered trademarks of International Business Machines Corporation in the United States and other countries.

Java, JavaBeans, JavaScript, JavaServer, JDBC, JDK, 100% Pure Java, Solaris, and Write Once, Run Anywhere are trademarks or registered trademarks of Sun Microsystems, Inc. ActiveX, Microsoft, Windows, and Windows NT are trademarks or registered trademarks of Microsoft Corporation. Other company, product, and service names may be trademarks or service marks of their respective companies or organizations.

All rights reserved. No part of this book may be reproduced, in any form or by any means, without permission in writing from the publisher.

Printed in the United States of America
10   9   8   7   6   5   4   3   2

ISBN 0-13-022475-8

Prentice-Hall International (UK) Limited, *London*
Prentice-Hall of Australia Pty. Limited, *Sydney*
Prentice-Hall Canada Inc., *Toronto*
Prentice-Hall Hispanoamericana, S.A., *Mexico*
Prentice-Hall of India Private Limited, *New Delhi*
Prentice-Hall of Japan, Inc., *Tokyo*
Prentice-Hall (Singapore) Pte. Ltd., *Singapore*
Editora Prentice-Hall do Brasil, Ltda., *Rio de Janeiro*

Contents

v

Chapter 4
Security, 61

Chapter 5
Persistence, 71

Chapter 6
Transaction Management, 77

Chapter 7
Development and Deployment, 93

Chapter 8

The Future of Enterprise JavaBeans, 99

Chapter 9

Technology, 105

List of Figures

Preface

Dear Reader,

You have begun a book that is unique in many ways. First, the team who wrote this book are IBM and external technical professionals from countries around the globe. They were part of a short project exploring the new component architecture of Enterprise JavaBeans.

Second, this publication is meant to smoothly connect theoretical and practical elements into one natural flow; in doing this, the book will easily find its home on the bookshelves of architects and consultants, and, likewise, it could find its place on the desk of developers to guide them through their first steps in the implementation of this new architecture.

This book goes beyond the technical value of Java and JavaBeans and looks at adding real business value to an enterprise.

IBM, Sun, and several other vendors have worked together to create the Enterprise JavaBeans (EJB) specification. With this specification, developers can create server-side business components in Java, suitable for use in industrial-strength object-oriented and multitiered applications. This means Java components receive full life-cycle support and can participate in transactions and interoperate with resource managers, such as database managers, in a secure fashion.

Extending the principles of its Java heritage, The EJB specification also incorporates the notion of "develop once, deploy anywhere." With EJBs, it becomes possible to create reusable server-side Java components that can be managed in the runtime environment of any vendor who provides EJB servers conforming to the specification.

The team who wrote this publication tried to answer "why, what, and how" questions in that order. So, after you have practical experience with the simple sample scenarios, you should have a solid understanding of Enterprise JavaBeans and be ready to study this fascinating technology more deeply.

We wish you good luck in this endeavor.

The Team That Wrote This Book

The Jalapeño Team

This book was produced by a team of specialists from around the world, working at the International Technical Support Organization, Austin Center.

Henri Jubin is currently working for the International Technical Support Organization (ITSO) in Austin where he covers the area of Object-Oriented Technology. Henri has previously worked in various support and consulting positions within IBM France. He has dealt with topics such as object-oriented technology and OS/2.

Jürgen Friedrichs is a project leader in the OO/AD group at the International Technical Support Organization (ITSO), Austin Center. In the past year, Jürgen led various Java projects in the ITSO. Before joining the ITSO in 1997, Jürgen worked in Technical Marketing Support for OS/2, Warp Server, and TCP/IP in Germany.

Douglas Kosovic is a Research and Development Engineer at DSTC Pty Ltd (Distributed Systems Technology Centre) in Brisbane, Australia. He coauthored the initial and revised specification submission for OMG's *DCE/CORBA Interworking RFC*. Douglas wrote all CORBA clients and servers (including those for IBM DSOM) in the CORBAnet showcase (see `http://www.corba.net`) that was sponsored by the OMG to demonstrate ORB interoperability. Currently, he is writing and enhancing a Java code generator that creates Java CORBA servers on-demand from a user-supplied MOF (OMG's Meta Object Facility) description.

Thea Hygh is a Consulting I/T Specialist for IBM Advanced Technical Support, Dallas Systems Center, located in Roanoke, Texas. He specializes in transaction systems, particularly for distributed transaction processing environments. He has 25 years of experience with development and deployment of customer application solutions, using IBM transaction processing systems such as CICS, Transaction Server, and TXSeries.

Daniel Fischer is an IT project leader in the Application Services group of IBM Global Services, Switzerland. He specializes in Object Technology and Application Architectures. Daniel holds a BSC in Computer Science and has 12 years of experience in application development.

Rashik Parmar is the client consultant responsible for IBM's technical relationship with a large UK financial institution. During the 15 years of practical experience in IBM, Rashik has worked for financial, retail, and manufacturing clients on projects of all sizes. Overall, he specializes in, and ensures, the technical success of complex IT projects. He has both a wide breadth and depth of knowledge in IT systems acquired through various technical specialist roles. Rashik has directed the implementation of a wide range of solutions through to the realization of the business benefits. His projects have ranged from replacement branch systems to consolidation of core systems following business mergers. Recently, he designed the infrastructure for a number of object-oriented and Internet-based solutions.

Thanks to the following people for their invaluable contributions to this project.

Alex Gregor
IBM International Technical Support Organization, Austin Center

John Cook
IBM Austin, Technical / Architecture Lead for IBM Java Beans

Jim Knutson
IBM Austin, Bean Extender Technical Lead

David Morrill
IBM Austin, EJB Development

Temi Rose
IBM International Technical Support Organization, Austin Center
for her creative inspiration and for creating the graphics in this book

Comments Welcome

Your comments are important to us!

We want our book to be as helpful as possible. Please send us your comments about this book in one of the following ways:

- Use the electronic evaluation form found on the IBM Redbooks Web sites:

  For Internet users: `http://www.redbooks.ibm.com`

  For IBM Internet users: `http://w3.itso.ibm.com`

- Send us a note at the following address:

  `redbook@us.ibm.com`

Enterprise
JavaBeans™
by Example

Chapter 1

Why Enterprise JavaBeans?

▼ THE NEED FOR ENTERPRISE JAVABEANS

▼ BUILDING APPLICATIONS FROM COMPONENTS

▼ THE MULTITIER PARADIGM

▼ THE ENTERPRISE JAVABEANS COMPONENT MODEL

Enterprise JavaBeans has generated a tremendous amount of interest since the first release of the specification in March 1998. The specification defines the Enterprise JavaBeans architecture and outlines an Application Programming Interface (API) that will enable developers, using Java technology, to build platform-independent, mission-critical, server-side applications. The EJB Specification is comprehensive, attempting to meet a number of goals and objectives. Briefly, the specification defines and discusses distinct roles for the development and deployment of Enterprise JavaBeans, describes how EJB interoperates with clients and existing systems, specifies the EJB compatibility with the Common Object Request Broker Architecture (CORBA), and defines the responsibilities for the various components in the system.

As part of the specification, Sun provides the following description.

> *The Enterprise JavaBeans architecture is a component architecture for the development and deployment of object-oriented distributed enterprise-level applica-*

1

tions. Applications written using the Enterprise JavaBeans architecture are scalable, transactional, and multi-user secure. These applications may be written once, and then deployed on any server platform that supports the Enterprise Java-Beans specification.

Source: *Sun Microsystems Enterprise JavaBeans Version 1.0 Specification, March 21, 1998*

According to Sun, "The Enterprise JavaBeans Application Programming Interface will give enterprise developers and solution providers a new strategic weapon to build the next generation of industrial strength, mission-critical business applications." Although you may be familiar with Sun's Java platform or Java Development Kit (JDK) for development of client-side applications, you may not be aware that Sun has recently defined a server-based platform for Java-based enterprise computing. This server platform was described as part of a Java for the Enterprise initiative, which was unveiled by Sun at the JavaOne Conference in April 1997. The initiative was announced as a collaborative effort, with endorsement by several partners, including Baan, BEA, IBM, Informix, Netscape, Novell, Oracle, Sybase, Symantec, and Tandem. It consists of a set of standardized APIs for enterprise-level distributed Java applications and a set of extensions to the JavaBeans architecture to allow enterprise applications to easily participate in important enterprise services. The Java Platform for the Enterprise and associated APIs are depicted in Figure 1–1.

These APIs enable client and server applications, applets, and servlets to access common server-side systems and subsystems. This approach facilitates the creation, deployment, and management of scalable Java business applications. This architecture allows application developers to focus on their business logic without having to worry about the infrastructure that makes the server environment so complex today. In Figure 1–1, JMAPI refers to the Java Management API, which defines access to a set of services for managing Java resources. JNDI, the Java Naming and Directory Interface, is an API for accessing naming and directory services. JTS is the Java Transaction Service, an API for invoking transaction services. JIDL refers to Java Interface Definition Language, an interface to the CORBA set of services for distributed computing. JMS, the Java Message Service, is an API for invoking asynchronous message delivery services. Finally, JDBC, the Java Database Connectivity API, enables access to data in existing databases through a common interface.

The centerpiece of Java Platform for the Enterprise is Enterprise JavaBeans, a Java model for software components that encapsulates business logic and runs on an application server. The Enterprise JavaBeans component architecture is designed to enable enterprises to build scalable, secure, multiplatform, business-critical

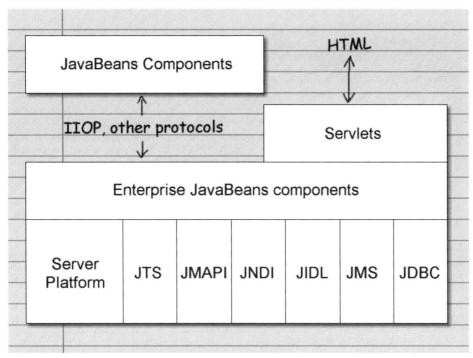

Figure 1-1 *Java Platform for the Enterprise*

applications as reusable, server-side components. This book describes the implications and architecture of the EJB component model and presents realistic examples of how EJB components work.

The Need for Enterprise JavaBeans

So, why do we need Enterprise JavaBeans? Surely there is a plethora of existing technologies, frameworks, and architectures, so what's new about Enterprise Java-Beans? To answer these questions, we need to explore the problems that developers face today. Then, let us look through some of the developments that have occurred over the last few years to culminate in the creation of Enterprise JavaBeans.

Businesses around the world are being forced to change faster to keep pace with market forces. These, in turn, require new or changed information technology (IT) systems. Enterprise application developers are forced to create new applications or extend existing IT systems in an ever-shorter time to accommodate new business processes or changes in the business models.

Hardly any development projects today start from scratch. New applications usually have to tightly integrate with existing core IT systems. Many of the existing applications are over 20 years old. They have been modified so many times that they have usually lost their structure and are no longer comprehensible. This situation is made more complex by the need to integrate systems across heterogeneous environments. Finally, the applications often must be distributed across multiple platforms, that is, to live in multiple pieces on a network of heterogeneous servers, and must execute in a guaranteed, reliable fashion.

In the past, application developers tried to create all-encompassing, single-block applications (so-called bloatware). These applications tried to handle every possible requirement the developer could conceive. Such applications quickly became hard to develop, difficult to maintain, and almost impossible to adapt to future needs in a reasonable amount of time.

Application developers are responding to these demands by producing reusable and flexible software parts or components. They are looking to find ways in which software components can be purchased, rapidly customized, and integrated into heterogeneous multitier platforms. They want one version of these components to run unchanged on all of their platforms.

Organizations do not want to be locked into a single vendor or provider of IT systems. They want to have choice and want to use market forces to increase competition among component manufacturers, as is the case with hardware components today. This flexibility will provide users with a better choice of software components and will also lower IT costs. For this desired result to become a reality, the components must be deployable on all available platforms.

The Enterprise JavaBeans technology is the computer industry's collaborative response, addressing the challenges that application developers face around the world. Enterprise JavaBeans defines a component model for building and deploying Java applications from reusable, server-side application components. It defines the architecture for the components, the environment to support the components, and the method to develop, deploy, and reuse the components. The components are designed to be multitier, multiplatform, and able to support the demands of business-critical applications.

To better understand the value of Enterprise JavaBeans, let us now look at two core industry themes: building applications from components and multitier applications. These themes are brought together in the final section, which provides an overview of the Enterprise JavaBeans component model.

Building Applications from Components

The first of the core industry themes is building applications from components. Component technology promises a world in which customized business solutions can be assembled from a set of off-the-shelf software components. The proposition is that independent software vendors produce specialized components for various business problems or requirements. Examples for the banking industry might be components for a sales aid for the bank's sales representatives, a customer folder, and a savings account. Enterprises simply select the appropriate components that best match their business needs and assemble them into a working solution.

A component model defines the basic architecture of a component-based system, specifying the structure of its interfaces and the mechanisms by which it interacts with its environment. The component model provides guidelines to create and implement components that can operate together to form a larger application. These guidelines allow application builders to combine components from different developers or different vendors to construct an application.

Figure 1–2 shows an example of an application built from components. In this example, components from three packages — A and B from Pkg1, C and B from Pkg2, and E and F from Pkg3 — have been combined with two in-house components A and B by a vendor C. So, unlike the past situation wherein a purchased package had to be implemented in total, the component approach allows elements from multiple packages to be combined.

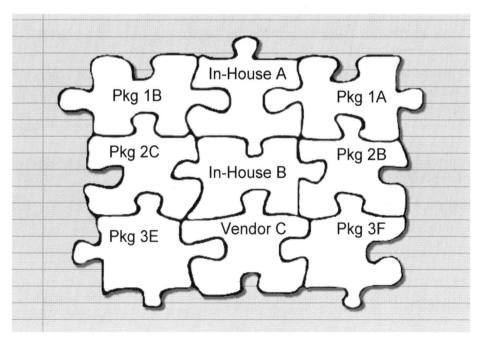

Figure 1–2 *An Application Built from Components*

So, What Is a Component?

A component is a reusable software building block that has a defined and published interface and provides application functionality. Components can be combined with other components and "glue code" to rapidly produce a custom application.

What Are Server Components?

Server components are application components that run on a server. As we explain in the next section, most of an application's logic is moving from the client to one or more servers in a multitier application architecture. These components implement small requirements and are designed to be combined with other components of the same architecture to form a total solution.

A server component model simplifies the process of moving logic to the server. It also helps in splitting the application into various well-defined logical components to accommodate reuse, scalability, and performance requirements.

What Does the Component Environment Provide?

Component builders want to concentrate on creating the business logic. They do not want to develop the environment for the component, that is, support for multithreading, concurrency control, resource management, security, and transaction management. If these services were implemented differently by each component, achieving portability and interoperability between components from different vendors would be very difficult, if not impossible, to accomplish.

The component environment provides runtime services by means of component containers. The container insulates the component from the runtime platform and manages the shared use of resources, such as execution threads, memory, and CPU. When a client invokes a server component, the container automatically allocates the needed resources and initiates the component. The container manages all interactions between the component and the external systems. Figure 1–3 illustrates the component environment.

How Do We Get Plug-and-Play Assembly?

The ultimate goal for component-based systems is to achieve plug-and-play assembly. In other words, developers should be able to purchase a component, install it, and integrate it into their system with minimal or no effort. A component model makes this goal possible by standardizing the contracts (interfaces) by which components interact with each other and their runtime environment. These standard interfaces enable a high level of integration and interoperability. They also enable faster application development and allow the use of visual component assembly tools.

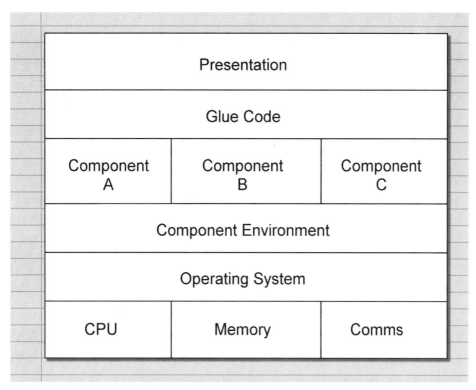

Figure 1–3 *Component Environment*

What's the Market Acceptance of Component-Based Development?

So far, there is a fairly rich supply of off-the-shelf, third-party components for the client side. The market for server-side components is still very young. As more organizations adopt the server component architecture model, the market is likely to grow rapidly. Software companies, such as IBM, are already beginning to implement applications by using server-side components. We expect companies to begin to sell individual server components in the near future.

The Multitier Paradigm

The second core industry theme is the multitier paradigm. Multitier applications provide a number of significant advantages, including scalability, reliability, manageability, reusability, and flexibility, over traditional client/server architectures. Enterprise JavaBeans defines a component model that supports multitier, distributed object applications. Let's look at multitier applications in a little more detail.

Partitioning Applications

The client/server systems have been commonly used to exploit the processing power of workstations to provide more user-friendly and responsive systems. In traditional client/server applications, the client application can contain any or all of the presentation logic (the graphical user interface), application navigation, the business logic (algorithms and business rules), and data manipulation logic (database access). This kind of application is commonly called a fat client. The server is generally a (distributed) database management system or a transaction monitor, which is actually not a part of the application itself. We call this a two-tier architecture. Figure 1–4 shows the range of different client/server implementations that are possible. Because of this range of possible implementations, the integration of different client systems and server systems is often complex and requires significant programming effort.

In a multitier architecture, the client application usually contains only presentation logic, which may include some very simple control and plausibility check

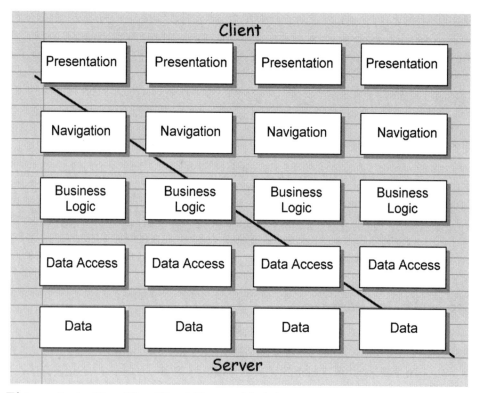

Figure 1–4 *Two-Tier Client/Server Models*

logic. We call this kind of application a thin client. The business logic and data access logic are spread over one or more separate components running on one or more application servers. These business application components, in turn, access enterprise data on backend systems, usually called data servers. Hence, the term multitier application. The application has been partitioned and deployed onto three or more interacting tiers, each providing unique functionality to the application.

Tier 1 The client providing the presentation logic (the GUI)

Tier 2 The application server providing the business logic (that is, the business processes) and often the associated integration middleware

Tier 3 The data server providing the business data

Figure 1–5 shows an example of a three-tier system.

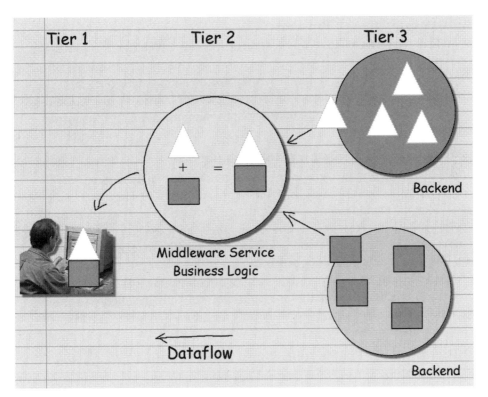

Figure 1-5 *Three-Tier Client/Server Architecture*

What Is the Value of Multitier Applications?

Moving the business and data manipulation logic to the server allows an application to take advantage of the power of high-end, multithreaded, and multiprocessing systems. Server components can pool and share scarce resources, such as processes, threads, memory, database connections, and so on.

Multitier Systems Are Scalable

As system demands increase, highly active components can be distributed across multiple servers. Although modern client/server systems can easily support hundreds of concurrent users, their scalability is limited. Partitioning or replicating data among distributed servers brings some relief from the common bottlenecks of centralized data management, but it does not provide the desired application performance while keeping the cost per user low.

Multitier systems can be built with almost no scalability limits. Additional upgrades can always be made to the environment to boost performance and to support additional users. Multitier systems can scale to support hundreds of thousands of concurrent users.

Multitier Systems Are Reliable

The multitier approach allows applications to be very reliable and to provide a consistent level of service. This is achieved by implementing multiple levels of redundancy. Replication and distribution of critical components onto multiple servers can eliminate bottlenecks and single points of failure. Typically, the run-time environment automatically takes care of synchronization and concurrency implications.

Multitier Systems Are Manageable and Secure

Thin-client applications are generally easier to manage than traditional client/server applications because very little application code (if any) is actually deployed on the client systems. Most of the application logic is installed, managed, and maintained on servers. Fixes, upgrades, and extensions, as well as new versions, can all be administered through a centralized management environment. The Java model even supports transparent downloading of the client part of an application at startup time. This feature not only increases the reliability of server-side applications compared to applications directly installed on a client system but also enables stricter security policies through enforced security controlling mechanisms on the server.

Multitier Systems Enable Reusability and Simplified Integration

Server components are accessed and managed through well-defined interfaces. By the nature of these interfaces, a server component is a reusable software building block. Each component implements a specific set of functions that are published and made accessible to any other component or application through that interface. A particular business function can be implemented once and then be reused in any applications that require the function.

If an organization maintains a comprehensive library of components, application development becomes more and more a matter of assembling the appropriate components into a system that performs the required business functions.

The Enterprise JavaBeans Component Model

The Enterprise JavaBeans component model is a culmination of the core industry themes into a new model for developing and deploying systems. It defines a model for multitier Java software components. You are probably aware of JavaBeans and might be wondering, "How does Enterprise JavaBeans relate to JavaBeans?" Although the two architectures have JavaBeans in their name, that is where the similarity ends. JavaBeans is the component model for Java, whereas Enterprise JavaBeans describes a server framework model for distributed Java components. Let's look at the JavaBeans component model in a little more detail before we move on.

JavaBeans Component Model

According to its inventors at Sun Microsystems, "A JavaBean is a reusable software component that can be manipulated visually using a builder tool."

The JavaBeans model is the definition of a uniform and flexible Java software component model made for easy manipulation in visual development tools. It defines the APIs needed for intercomponent communication through events and methods, utilization of properties, customization of Beans at development time, and persistence by use of the Java streaming mechanism. The JavaBeans specification defines core JavaBeans features such as events, event registration, properties, and introspection. These are not even mentioned by the Enterprise JavaBeans specifications.

The JavaBeans architecture is commonly regarded as a component model for the client side. Although JavaBeans are widely used for GUI programming, they can be used equally well for any kind of server-side (nonvisual) programming. But JavaBeans models fall far short of meeting enterprise computing requirements. They do not offer any kind of standardized, built-in infrastructure access API for services, such as remote accessibility, life-cycle management, transaction management, and security. Although it is always possible to code these kinds of services directly into a Bean, such an attempt results in an inflexible, and probably nonportable, solution. This is where the Enterprise JavaBeans architecture comes in.

The Enterprise JavaBeans Model

The Enterprise JavaBeans component model is defined as an object architecture for component-based, transaction-oriented, distributed enterprise computing. The model, as is shown in Figure 1–6, defines four key elements — the server (which provides the transaction management and security), the container in which the Enterprise JavaBeans will execute, the interface to client systems, and finally, the interface to backend systems and databases.

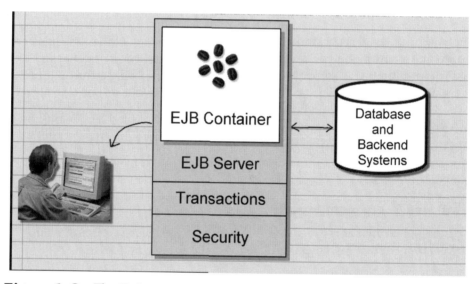

Figure 1–6   *The Enterprise JavaBeans Framework Model*

The emphasis of this architecture is to define a framework in which Java components can be deployed. Consequently, there is no mention of events or properties because Enterprise JavaBeans has other means to communicate and manage state. A process for deploying the Beans is also defined to allow customization to be handled at deployment time rather than at development time. The Enterprise JavaBeans model further defines various development roles and scenarios. This model clearly defines all the stages in creating and implementing an Enterprise JavaBeans-based application. It allows different organizations to create the servers, the containers, and the packages of Beans. It allows an organization to take a number of packages of Beans and create applications. And, this model also supports higher-level visual development tools, giving developers benefits similar to those of the JavaBeans model.

When using JavaBeans to create a full-scale server application, developers have to build the entire framework around it. They need to create their own mechanisms for managing transactions, for sharing resources, security, and performance. With the Enterprise JavaBeans framework, these mechanisms are provided by an Enterprise server provider. Developers can then concentrate on creating the business logic. By use of the EJB model, valuable development time is saved and components are highly portable to any EJB server.

Now, let us look in more detail at the elements of the Enterprise JavaBean model. We start by looking at the Beans themselves ("The Enterprise Java Beans" on page 13), then move on to the container and the server ("The Server and Container: The Execution Engine" on page 15), and, finally, we look at developing and deploying EJBs ("Packaging and Deployment" on page 17).

The Enterprise Java Beans

In this section, we describe the characteristics of Enterprise JavaBeans implementations — Enterprise Java Beans.

Transaction Management — an Integral Part of EJBs

By default, Enterprise Java Beans are transaction aware. Although Enterprise Java Beans can be used to implement nontransactional systems, the model was designed for distributed transactions. Enterprise Java Beans require the use of a distributed transaction management system in order to manage the two-phase commit protocol for distributed flat transactions. Enterprise JavaBeans transactions are based on a subset of the Java Transaction Service (JTS) API. JTS is the Java binding for the CORBA Object Transaction Service (OTS). JTS supports distributed transactions that can span multiple databases on multiple systems coordinated by multiple transaction managers. By using JTS, an Enterprise JavaBeans server ensures that its transactions can interoperate with other Enterprise Java-Beans servers.

The Enterprise JavaBeans model also supports implicit transactions. Individual Enterprise Java Beans do not need to specify transaction demarcation code to participate in distributed transactions. The execution environment automatically manages the start, commit, and rollback of transactions on behalf of the Beans. Transaction policies can be defined as part of the deployment process. Optionally, transactions can be controlled by the client application.

Persistence — Connecting to Databases and Backend Systems

Enterprise JavaBeans provides a simple programming model for managing object persistence. The EJB architecture model defines entity objects that are the means to integrate with backend systems and databases. An entity object can manage its own persistence, or it can delegate its persistence to its container. Persistence functions must be performed whenever objects are created or destroyed or whenever objects are loaded or deleted from memory. The Enterprise JavaBeans model supports the following two persistence mechanisms.

- **Bean-Managed Persistence.** If the entity object is to manage its own persistence, then the Enterprise JavaBean developer must implement persistence operations (for example, JDBC or JSQL calls) directly in the Enterprise JavaBeans class methods. If the implementation is not done properly (that is, by using a proprietary interface), the Bean may not be portable. Also, this mechanism usually ties an Enterprise Java Bean to a specific type of datastore (that is, a relational database).

- **Container-Managed Persistence.** If the entity object delegates persistence services, the EJB container transparently and implicitly manages the persistence state. The Bean developer does not need to provide any code for data source access within the Enterprise Java Bean itself. Thus, the Bean is completely independent of any specific type of data source. The container provider's tools generate the code that will be used to implement the persistence process.

Ever since the first release of the Enterprise JavaBeans, the specification has not defined how the EJB container must manage object persistence; it is highly vendor specific. Vendors can implement anything from very basic to very sophisticated persistence services in their EJB containers. Container-specific tools will be provided to map the Enterprise JavaBeans fields to the data source at deployment time.

Policy-Based Security Services — Building the Java Mechanisms

The Enterprise JavaBeans model builds on the standard Java security services supported in the Java Development Kit (JDK) 1.1.x. Java security supports authentication and authorization services to restrict access to secure objects and methods. Users (people, departments, companies, organizations, and so on) are represented by Identity objects. Users can be authenticated by means of a credential (that is, password, certificate, public key, and so on). Users can also assume the identity of other users to act on their behalf. Objects and methods are secured by a `SecurityDescriptor` identifying users that have access to the object or method.

Enterprise JavaBeans automates the use of Java security so that Enterprise JavaBeans do not need to code to the Java Security API directly. The security rules for each Enterprise Java Bean are defined in the `SecurityDescriptor`. The EJB container uses the `SecurityDescriptor` to automatically perform security checking on behalf of the Enterprise Java Bean.

The Server and Container: The Execution Engine

The runtime environment for the Enterprise Java Beans is provided by a combination of the server and the container. Let's start with the server. The Enterprise Java-Beans server (EJB server) provides a standard set of services for the container. Enterprise JavaBeans can be transactional. Therefore, the EJB server provides a distributed transaction management service. The EJB server must also provide at least one container for the Enterprise Java Beans, called an Enterprise JavaBeans container (EJB container). The EJB container implements the management and control services for one or more classes of Enterprise JavaBeans objects. It must provide life-cycle management (that is, from creation to destruction), implicit transaction control, persistence management, transparent distribution services, and security services for the Enterprise JavaBean. Figure 1–7 illustrates the execution environment.

In most circumstances, a single vendor would provide both an EJB server and an associated EJB container, although the specification allows the separation of these services. The implementation of services, such as process management, thread-pooling, concurrency control, and resource management is not defined within the

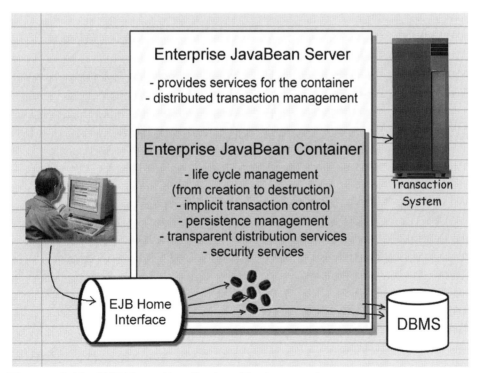

Figure 1-7 *EJB Execution System Environment*

scope of the Enterprise JavaBeans specification. Individual vendors can differentiate their products by the simplicity or the sophistication of these services.

The EJB container completely insulates the Enterprise JavaBeans developer from platform-dependent APIs, such as a specific middleware or an operation environment. All the developer sees and is concerned about is an interface called EJB home. This is the interface used by clients and other Enterprise Java Beans. This architectural independence from an application and its runtime environment allows the EJB server vendor or EJB container vendor to improve and change the middleware layer without impacting existing applications.

A Standards-Based Scalable Platform

The Enterprise JavaBeans model is based on industry-standard protocols, such as TCP/IP, the Internet Inter-ORB Protocol (IIOP), and even DCOM. The specification does not mandate any wire protocol. This diversity implies that clients and remote components do not have to be written in pure Java.

The model is appropriate for small-scale applications to large-scale business transaction systems. As business requirements grow, existing applications can migrate progressively to more powerful operating environments without modification.

The environment supports Internet-based applications through simple connection mechanisms with Web servers as well as with a variety of other Internet-enabled client devices. Interoperability with heterogeneous clients is provided either through Java bridging mechanisms or directly through the EJB-to-CORBA mapping and the IIOP protocol support. The CORBA mapping not only enables interoperability among multiple vendors' EJB servers and client implementations but also allows the propagation of the transaction and security contexts through the standard CORBA object services.

Transparent attachment to various vendor-specific backend systems is provided by the EJB containers. Most relational database systems can be accessed directly through the JDBC API if required.

The Enterprise JavaBeans model enables a much higher level of integration and interoperability than ever before. Enterprise JavaBeans applications can be developed in any Enterprise JavaBeans-compliant environment, and users can deploy the applications in any other EJB-compliant environment. As requirements for higher performance, increased scalability, or tighter security arise, the Beans can be moved to an environment with more comprehensive and sophisticated services. Applications implemented with Enterprise JavaBeans can be deployed on a much broader array of systems than can any other software component model available today. In addition, EJBs can be easily customized and integrated with existing application systems.

Paving the Way to Component Portability

As we have discussed so far, the Enterprise JavaBeans architecture provides a simple and elegant server/container component model. The model ensures that the Beans can be developed once and deployed in any vendor's container system. Even though the various container systems may implement their runtime services differently, the Enterprise JavaBeans interfaces ensure that a Bean can rely on the underlying system to provide consistent life cycle, persistence, transaction, distribution, and security services. These services effectively implement a portability layer. Therefore, any Enterprise Java Bean can run in any application execution system that supports the specifications. This paves the way for organizations to develop and sell server components or packages. Users will be able to buy these packages and be able to easily integrate them with existing database and backend systems.

Simplified Customization: The Key to Ease of Implementation

Enterprise JavaBeans applications are highly customizable. The underlying Java-Beans component model supports customization without even requiring access to source code. Application behaviors and runtime settings can be defined through a set of Bean properties that can be changed at development or deployment time. For example, a property might be used to specify the location of a database or to specify a default language at deployment time.

Packaging and Deployment

Enterprise JavaBeans can be packaged as individual Enterprise Java Beans, as a collection of Enterprise Java Beans, or as a complete application system. Enterprise Java Beans are distributed in a *Java Archive file* (called an EJB Jar file). The EJB Jar file contains information outlining the contents of the file, the Enterprise JavaBeans class files, a Deployment/Descriptor telling the EJB container how to manage and control the Enterprise Java Bean, and, optionally, the environment properties files.

The various settings in the Deployment/Descriptor can be defined either at application assembly or deployment time. Here is a summary of what is included in the Deployment/Descriptor.

Life Cycle	Defines how to create and maintain an Enterprise JavaBean object
Persistence	Indicates whether the object manages its own persistence or delegates persistence to its container
Transactions	Specifies what transaction semantics should be applied to the Enterprise Java Bean
Security	Identifies the security rules that should be applied to the Enterprise Java Bean

Industry Support

The industry has shown a lot of support for the Enterprise JavaBeans initiative. Most major vendors — including IBM, Oracle, Sybase, Netscape, BEA Systems, and others — have participated in the definition of the Enterprise JavaBeans specification. These vendors and others have indicated plans to implement support for Enterprise JavaBeans in their products. Enterprise JavaBeans technology builds and integrates on top of established enterprise systems that are already used by many companies today. Therefore, it gives a high level of investment protection to both EJB technology vendors as well as adopters.

The following list numbers just a few product families that either support the Java enterprise component model already or will be extended to support a container for Enterprise JavaBeans in the future. The list is not comprehensive — new products are emerging quickly as the Enterprise JavaBeans model is embraced by the IT industry on a broad scale.

- TP monitors, such as BEA Tuxedo and IBM TXSeries (CICS and Encina)

- Component Transaction Servers, such as IBM Component Broker Connector (CB-Connector), Sybase Jaguar CTS, and Microsoft Transaction Server

- CORBA platforms, such as Borland VisiBroker/ITS, IBM CB-Connector, and Iona Orbix/OTM

- Web platforms, such as IBM WebSphere Application Server (WAS) in conjunction with Enterprise Server for Java (ESJ), and Netscape Application Server

- Database management systems, such as IBM DB2, Oracle, and Sybase

Conclusion

Enterprise JavaBeans moves us closer to the world of component-based enterprise computing. It makes possible modern approaches for building new applications, such as usable and portable server-side components. It allows applications to be partitioned into multiple tiers to achieve better performance, scalability, reliability, and reusability compared with traditional client/server applications.

Chapter **2**

EJB Architecture Elements

▼ EJB ARCHITECTURE ELEMENTS — A FIRST GLANCE

▼ UNDERSTANDING ENTERPRISE JAVABEANS

▼ THE CLIENT'S VIEW OF AN EJB

▼ EJB CONTAINERS

▼ THE EJB SERVER ENVIRONMENT

This chapter covers the key elements and core characteristics of the Enterprise JavaBeans architecture as defined by the JavaSoft EJB specification 1.0.

We start by explaining what an Enterprise JavaBeans software component is and elaborate in depth on the two basic types of Enterprise Java Beans, the Session and Entity Bean. After that, we have a closer look at the relevant EJB interfaces from a client's perspective. Next, we explain the Bean's runtime and management environment, and the Enterprise JavaBeans container (subsequently referred to as container). Finally, we introduce the most important aspects of the container's runtime environment and the EJB server. After finishing this chapter, you should have a good understanding of the architectural concepts and elements that make up Enterprise JavaBeans.

19

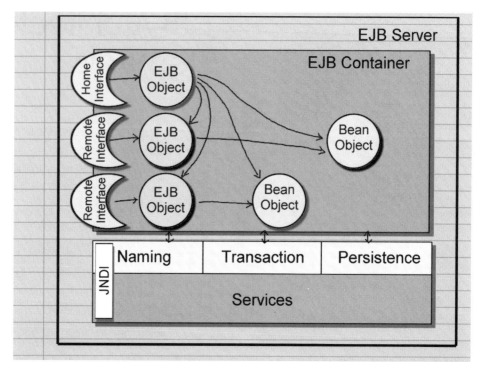

Figure 2-1 *EJB Core Elements*

EJB Architecture Elements — A First Glance

Figure 2–1 illustrates the core elements defined by the EJB architecture. The figure reveals the associations between the elements and the most important interfaces for the client.

The EJB Server is the outermost container of the various elements making up an EJB environment. The server manages one or more EJB containers and provides the required support services, such as transaction management, persistence, and client access. A JNDI-accessible naming space can be used by clients to locate the Enterprise JavaBeans. The server also provides the operation resources, such as processes and execution threads, memory, networking facilities, and so on, to the containers and their elements within. The EJB Server can offer further vendor-specific features, such as optimized database access drivers, interfaces to backend systems, or CORBA accessibility.

The EJB container is an abstract facility that manages one or more EJB classes and their instances. The container makes the required services accessible to the Beans through interfaces defined in the specification. A container vendor may also provide additional services implemented either in the container or in the server. Note that there is currently no interface defined between the container and the EJB server. This issue will be addressed in release 2 of the EJB specification.

The home interface lists the available methods for creating, destroying, and locating Enterprise Java Beans in the container. The home object is the implementation of the home interface that is specific to a container.

The remote interface defines the business methods offered by an Enterprise Java-Beans class. Note that this interface is not directly implemented by the Bean class but by an EJBObject class that mediates the client's calls to a Bean object.

Additional interfaces defined in the EJB specification allow Beans to interact with the transaction service and control persistence if they are designed to do so. For simplicity, these interfaces are not shown in Figure 2–1.

The term Enterprise JavaBeans may have several different meanings depending on the reader's point of view and prime interest or line of business. For a domain IT architect, for example, the term may describe the overall Enterprise Java component architecture. A container provider may interpret Enterprise JavaBeans primarily as a specification for a Java component framework, whereas a Bean developer might possibly understand it as the guideline for writing Enterprise JavaBeans components and the definition of their interfaces. In effect, the specification covers all the views mentioned above and interrelates them to various development and deployment roles and processes.

Understanding Enterprise JavaBeans

In this section, we primarily look at the elements within the container, the EJB classes and instances, in short — the Beans.

In addition to defining the EJB runtime infrastructure, the EJB architecture addresses two distinct models for building distributed applications. In the first model, the client interacts with a server object, which acts like an application, executing a unit of work on behalf of the client. Additionally, this object can keep client-specific data that is private to the client's session, allowing state information or intermediate data to be memorized between individual method calls (but not across multiple sessions). This model is referred to as the Session Beans model. In the second model, the client accesses an object that represents a business data entity, such as a row within a database table. This model enables several clients to access the same entity in a save manner, that is, either by using transaction coordination or database locking mechanism or both. This model is referred to as the Entity Beans model.

The following bullets describe some of the common characteristics of the two types of Enterprise Java Beans.

- **Enterprise Java Beans Are Managed by a Container**

  An Enterprise JavaBeans instance is created and managed at runtime by its EJB container. Client access to the Bean is mediated by the container and the EJB server on which the Enterprise Java Bean is deployed. The container provides services, such as automatic transaction management, security enforcement, life-cycle management, and persistence, on behalf of the Bean. If an Enterprise Java Bean uses only the standard container services defined by the EJB specification, the Bean can be deployed in any compliant EJB container. Specialized containers may provide additional services beyond those defined by the EJB specification. An Enterprise Java Bean that depends on such services can be deployed only in a container that supports the additional services.

- **Beans Can Be Customized at Development and Deployment Time**

  Bean customization is supported through the deployment descriptor, which is an integral part of a Bean's packaging information. The deployment descriptor acts as a property sheet that can be defined and filled in by the developer. In addition to providing these environment properties for a Bean class, the deployment descriptor also contains detailed information about transaction modes and security attributes, which specify how a Bean will execute with respect to transactions and security.

  To allow customization at Bean installation time, attributes of the deployment descriptor packaged with the Bean can be modified at deployment time rather than at development time. Certain attributes, such as the access control list and environment-specific information, will likely be adjusted at installation time of a Bean class to allow the Bean to work in the specific environment it is being deployed to. Other attributes, such as the transaction mode, will be specified by the Bean developer because they are driven by implementation-specific characteristics a deployer might not know.

  Container vendors will provide tools to support customization at deployment time. These tools would typically be used to modify the attributes in the deployment descriptor prior to Bean installations.

- **Beans Are Highly Portable**

  A client's view of an Enterprise Java Bean is defined by the Bean developer and specified in the Bean's home and remote interface. These interfaces are unaffected by the container and the server in which the Bean is deployed. Likewise, the services offered by a container are also transparent to the Bean. If the Bean limits itself to use only the interfaces defined by the specification, it is guaranteed to run in any compliant EJB container, thus ensuring that both the Beans and their pure Java clients are "Write Once, Run Everywhere."

However, there are some factors that may limit portability. One of them is how a Bean accesses its environment, that is, a datastore, if it is not designed to use the appropriate container services or if a container does not offer the required services. (Note that an EJB container that complies with the EJB specification Version 1.0 is not required to support Entity Beans.) This factor will most likely limit the portability of a Bean to environments that offer the services in exactly the manner the Beans expect. In the case of database access, a Bean might be limited to run only in systems that provide a certain database driver.

Other than that, an Enterprise Java Bean will still be deployed in a different EJB environment without having direct access to its source code. At deployment time, the EJBs and their container's deployment tools generate the appropriate EJB proxy objects that are delegating and intermediating calls from the client between the container and the deployed Enterprise Java Bean. The necessary information is extracted from the EJB Jar's manifest file.

Session Enterprise JavaBeans

A Session Bean is an EJB object that represents a transient conversation with a client. Think of a Session Bean as a logical extension of the client program that runs on the server. It performs operations, such as executing a business function or manipulating data in a transaction-safe manner, on behalf of the client. An example of using a Session Bean might be a Shopping Cart Bean, where many customers (clients) can simultaneously buy articles, adding them to their private shopping cart.

A Session Bean is considered private to the client and cannot be shared with other clients. This allows the Bean to maintain client-specific session information, called conversational state. A Session Bean that maintains conversational state is called a stateful Session Bean, as opposed to a stateless Session Bean that does not hold conversational state across multiple method invocations.

The Bean is created by the client through its home interface and, in most cases, exists only for the duration of a client/server session. However, the client can save a handle to a Session Bean and later use the handle to reactivate the session. If the client saves the handle persistently, it can even reactivate the session after a shutdown and restart.

Session Beans can be transactional, but they are generally not recoverable following a system crash or container restart unless the programmer has taken special care about this or unless the container vendor provides specific functionality to achieve such a behavior transparently to the Bean. Session objects, such as cached data from a database, that need to maintain conversational state in a save manner must manage their own persistence synchronization with the datastore. The container manages the state of a session object only if it needs to be temporarily evicted from memory, but it is not required by the specification to provide any built-in support for session persistency.

Session Beans are invaluable for providing overall control of transactions across invocations of multiple methods in the same or different EJBs. Without Session Beans, it might be necessary for client application developers to understand the transactional requirements of the EJB classes they wish to use and to utilize client-demarcated transactions to provide transaction control. One major benefit of EJB is that an application developer can write applications without needing to know their transactional requirements. A Session Bean can be created to represent a business operation, and that Session Bean can control the transaction, making client-demarcated transactions unnecessary.

Session Bean Definition

A class that implements the `javax.ejb.SessionBean` interface defines a Session Bean. This interface is defined as follows.

```
public interface javax.ejb.SessionBean
      extends javax.ejb.EnterpriseBean {
   public void ejbActivate() throws RemoteException;
   public void ejbPassivate() throws RemoteException;
   public void ejbRemove() throws RemoteException;
   public void setSessionContext(SessionContext context)
      throws RemoteException;
}
```

`ejbActivate()`	Is used by the container to notify the Session Bean that it is about to be (re-)activated (that is, restored from secondary storage to memory).
`ejbPassivate()`	Is used by the container to notify the Session Bean that it is about to be passivated (that is, temporarily evicted from memory).
`ejbRemove()`	Notifies the Bean that the container is about to end its life and that the Bean, therefore, should free all resources it holds.
`setSessionContext()`	Passes the reference to the Bean's session context for later reference. The session context provides access to the instances' context maintained by the container.

The `javax.ejb.EnterpriseBean` is the supertype for both Session and Entity Beans. It is an empty interface; that is, it does not define any methods, but it defines itself to be serializable so that the container can activate or passivate Enterprise Java Beans.

Stateful Session Beans

A stateful Session Bean is defined as a Session Bean that contains conversational state that must be retained across multiple method calls and transactions. The conversational state includes the Bean's field values and the transitive closure, that is, all referenced objects that would be stored by serializing the Bean's instance.

The conversational state can even contain open resources, such as open files, socket descriptors, or database connection, which cannot be saved when a Bean is evicted from memory. In these cases, the developer must close and reopen the resources by the `ejbPassivate()` and `ejbActivate()` methods, respectively.

The developer must also ensure that the conversational state is serializable, that is, every object either contained or referenced by a stateful Session Bean must implement the `java.io.Serializable` interface (which specifies any methods to be implemented). Also, note that the container is not required to reset the values of transient fields when activating a Bean. Therefore, using transient fields is generally discouraged unless the Bean can safely recover these fields in the `ejbActivate()` method.

A Session Bean's conversational state is not transactional; that is, the Bean's fields are not automatically restored to their initial state if the Bean's transaction rolls back. This restoration has to be taken care of by the developer through implementation of the `afterCompletion(boolean committed)` hook-method to manually restore the fields if the `committed` argument is passed as `false`. This method is defined by the optional `SessionSynchronization` interface and is called by the container when it completes a transaction either by committing it or rolling it back.

Stateless Session Beans

Stateless Session Beans are defined as Session Beans that do not maintain any conversational state across methods and transactions. An example is a Session Bean implementing pure algorithmic behavior in its business methods. This behavior implies that any Bean instance could be used by any client without the client knowing about it, allowing the container to manage stateless Beans in a more efficient way than their stateful counterparts. Because the stateless Beans can be used by any client, a container needs to retain only the number of Beans that are simultaneously used by active clients. Because of client think-time, this number is usually considerably smaller than the total number of clients holding a session. Thus, the container can minimize resources, such as memory for a large population of clients, by letting many clients transparently share the same Bean instance.

However, there are some implications.

- The home interface for a stateless Session Bean must have only one `create()` method that does not take any parameters, and the Session Bean class must define a single, no-arguments `ejbCreate()` method. This is probably the toughest limitation for a Bean developer.

- The `javax.ejb.SessionSynchronization` interface must not be implemented by a stateless Bean class. This is generally not a limitation because there is no conversation state to be synchronized with the transaction outcome.

- There is no fixed mapping between a stateless Bean and a client. The container simply delegates method calls to any available instance that is not running a method on behalf of another client. This is not a limitation because the client will never detect the delegation.

- Although the client may use the `create()` and `remove()` methods to control the Bean's life cycle, the container will likely ignore the calls and just provide a Bean that is currently not in use by another client.

Serialization of Method Calls

The container is responsible for serializing the calls to the methods of Session Beans, including method calls initiated by a client as well as the service callbacks made by the container. Therefore, a Session Bean's methods are not required to be reentered, that is, multiple threads are allowed to execute methods of the same Bean simultaneously. This rule eases the complexity of writing a Bean considerably, letting the developer concentrate on the business functionality without concern for concurrency issues. However, one implication of this rule is that it is illegal to make loopback calls; for example, Bean instance A calls a method on Bean instance B, which, in turn, calls back a method of instance A. This example would result in the container throwing the `java.rmi.RemoteException` at Bean instance B.

Entity Enterprise JavaBeans

The most common use for Entity Beans is to represent persistent data that is maintained either directly in a database or accessed through a backend application as an object. A simple Entity Bean could be defined to represent a single row in a database table, where each instance of the Bean represents a specific row. More-complex Entity Beans could represent views of joined tables in a database where one instance might represent a specific customer and all of that customer's orders and order items. There is no limitation to what an Entity Bean can represent as long as it fits the characteristics of Entity Beans.

Each entity object is identified by a unique identifier, which is generally implemented by the container using the entity's primary key. This identity survives a crash or restart of the container in which the Bean was created. Entity Bean instances can be created either by a factory object's `create()` method or by insertion of data directly into the underlying data source. Entity objects are transactional, and they are recoverable following a system crash.

Synchronizing Method Concurrency

In contrast to Session Beans, Entity Bean instances can be accessed simultaneously by multiple clients. However, it is the container's responsibility to properly synchronize the instance's state by using transactions. This delegation frees the developer from worrying about concurrent access from multiple transactions when writing the Bean's methods.

By default, an Entity Bean is not reentrant. If a method of a Bean instance is currently in execution, the container ensures that no other method is called on the same instance until the first one has completed. Also, the container ensures that the same method is not called concurrently on the same Bean by multiple threads of execution. Hence, a developer can code the Bean's methods for single-threaded use — a much easier and less error-prone task. However, this rule does not allow for loopback method calls in the same transaction contexts; for example, a Bean instance A calls a method on a Bean instance B, which, in turn, calls back a method on instance A.

In some circumstances, this limitation may be unacceptable. The container will enable loopback calls if the Bean's deployment descriptor explicitly indicates that the Bean is reentrant, that is, that a Bean's methods are able to share the current transaction, security, and execution contexts.

Reentrant Beans must be used with great caution because the container generally cannot distinguish a valid loopback call from illegal concurrent calls resulting from different clients. Also, concurrent calls in the same transaction context targeting the same Bean instance can lead to unpredictable results and are, therefore, considered illegal. Therefore, reentering should be avoided whenever possible, thus allowing the container to detect and prevent illegal concurrent calls from clients.

Managing Persistence

An entity object is considered implicitly persistent if it either manages its own persistence or delegates its persistence to the container. If an Entity Bean class provides for its own persistence, we call this Bean-managed persistence, as opposed to container-managed persistence, when the Bean delegates persistence to the container.

In the Bean-managed case, the Bean provider directly puts the database access code into the required Bean methods `ejbCreate()`, `ejbRemove()`, `ejbLoad()`, `ejbStore()`, and `ejbFind...()`. The advantage of using Bean-managed persistence is that it can be deployed in any container without having the container generate the database access calls. The main drawback is that the persistence is hard coded into the Bean, making it difficult to adapt the Bean to different types of datastores.

The container-managed case does not require any persistence code in the Bean's methods. Instead, the container provider's tools must generate the necessary functions at deployment time and implement them in the container. For the tools to generate the appropriate code, the developer must define all fields requiring persistence in the deployment descriptors `containerManagedFields` property. The main advantage of this method is that the Bean is completely independent of the datastore. A possible drawback is that the container vendor must provide sophisticated tools to support the generation of the datastore access code for all common types of data sources.

Defining an Entity Bean

An Entity Bean is created by defining a class that implements the `javax.ejb.EntityBean` interface. This interface is defined as follows.

```
public interface javax.ejb.EntityBean
      extends javax.ejb.EnterpriseBean {
   public void ejbLoad() throws RemoteException;
   public void ejbStore() throws RemoteException;
   public void ejbActivate() throws RemoteException;
   public void ejbPassivate() throws RemoteException;
   public void ejbRemove() throws RemoteException;
      throws RemoveException;
   public void setEntityContext(EntityContext context)
      throws RemoteException;
   public void unsetEntityContext() throws RemoteException;
}
```

ejbLoad()   Is called by the container to instruct the Bean instance to load its state from the underlying data source (only used with Bean-managed persistence).

`ejbStore()`	Is called before the container removes the entity object so that the Bean instance can synchronize the data source with its state (only used with Bean-managed persistence).
`ejbActivate()`	Is used by the container to notify the Bean instance that it is about to be (re-)activated (that is, restored from secondary storage to memory). The Bean can use this method to (re-)acquire necessary resources.
`ejbPassivate()`	Is used by the container to notify the Bean instance that it is about to be passivated (that is, temporarily evicted from memory). The Bean should release any resources that should not be held while the Bean is passivated.
`ejbRemove()`	Notifies the Bean instance that the container is about to remove it permanently and that the Bean, therefore, should free all resources it holds.
`setEntityContext()`	Passes the reference to the entity context to the Bean for later reference.
`unsetEntityContext()`	Removes the entity context from the Bean. This is the last method called on the Bean before it is destroyed by the container.

Comparison of Entity and Session Beans

It may occur to you that Session Beans might not be very useful, especially for database-driven applications. This perception is certainly not true. If an Entity Bean instance represents, for example, an underlying row in a database, the relationship between the Entity Bean instance and the database row is exactly one-to-one. If multiple clients must be able to access that underlying row, it means that, unlike Session Beans, the Entity Bean instances are to be shared among clients. Since they are shared, they should not allow storage of per-client state information. Session Beans, on the other hand, enable the client to store state information on behalf of the client. The relationship between the client and the Session Bean instance is always one-to-one.

An ideal solution might be a client that calls into the server through a Session Bean and the Session Bean accesses the data source through Entity Beans. This solution allows for storage of state information for both the client and for the rows in the database. Figure 2–2 illustrates this approach.

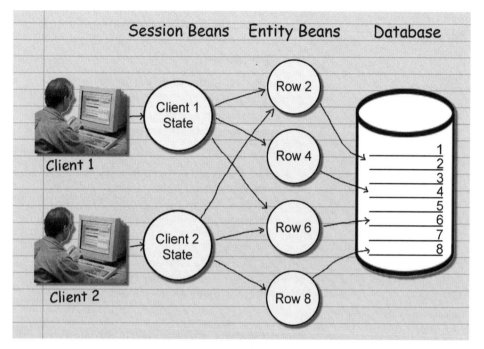

Figure 2–2   *Session and Entity Beans Relationship*

Creating and Removing Beans

Both creating and removing Bean objects, either through the home interface or through the Bean's remote interface, have different meanings for Entity and Session Beans.

Because Session Beans are not shareable between clients and usually vanish once a client terminates a session, the only way for a client to get a Session Bean is to create one. A client that requires access to an existing Entity Bean *finds* it by using the Bean's home interface (refer to "EJB Containers" on page 39 for a description of the home interface). Creating an Entity Bean implies that a new row should be inserted into the database. For this reason, creating an Entity Bean is not considered a part of the normal life cycle of an Entity Bean instance.

Removal of Session Beans means the Bean instance is removed from the container and cannot be used again (its state information is lost). For Entity Beans, removal means that the underlying row in the database should be deleted. Like the create operation, the remove operation is generally not considered part of the normal life cycle of an Entity Bean.

Be aware that support for Entity Beans by containers is optional in release 1.0 of the Enterprise JavaBeans specification, whereas support for session objects is required. The EJB 2.0 specification will require support for entity objects.

The Client's View of an EJB

This section explains a client's view of an Enterprise Java Bean. The EJB specification defines two types of interface the client developer typically uses: the remote interface and the home interface. These interfaces specify the contracts between the client and the container and between the client and the Beans in the container.

An Enterprise JavaBeans provider must define a *remote interface* that specifies the business functions the Bean offers to a client. The container is responsible for allowing the client to invoke the methods on the appropriate EJB objects by delegating the invocation to a Bean's instance, using a mediator object called EJBObject.

The second interface the Bean developer must provide is called the *home interface*. The home interface provides the means to create new EJB instances or to find existing ones (that is, by looking them up from a data source).

Figure 2–3 illustrates the two types of interfaces used by the client.

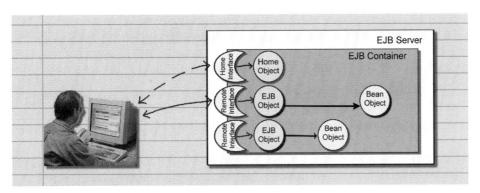

Figure 2–3   *The Client's View of an EJB*

The Remote Interface

The remote interface lists the business methods available to the client. It must be defined by the Enterprise JavaBean developer because the Bean must implement the appropriate functionality. A client never accesses the Enterprise JavaBean instances directly. Instead, the client uses the remote interface implemented by a remote object called the EJBObject. Note that it is the EJBObject class, not the Enterprise JavaBean class, that directly implements the remote interface.

The EJBObject

The client never gets a direct reference to the EJB object in the container. Instead, the container provides an EJBObject for the client as a mediator between the client, the container, and the EJB instance in the container. When the client invokes a method, the EJBObject receives the request and delegates it to the EJB instance, providing any necessary wrapper functionality and enabling the container to intercept the call in order to provide transaction management, security checks, or persistence-related tasks. To do all this, the EJBObject and the container must cooperate closely. Therefore, the container vendor should provide the means to generate a corresponding EJBObject at deployment time.

The EJBObject is the network-aware object, with a stub and skeleton, that acts as a proxy for the Bean. The Bean's remote interface, therefore, must extend the `EJBObject` interface, and the EJBObject class must implement this remote interface, making the EJBObject class specific to the Bean's class. For each Bean class, there will be a custom EJBObject class.

Here is the definition of the `EJBObject` interface, which the Bean's remote interface extends.

```
public interface javax.ejb.EJBObject extends java.rmi.Remote
  {
    public EJBHome getEJBHome() throws RemoteException;
    public Object getPrimaryKey() throws RemoteException;
    public Handle getHandle() throws RemoteException;
    public boolean isIdentical(EJBObject other)
        throws RemoteException;
    public void remove()
        throws RemoteException, RemoveException;
}
```

`getEJBHome()`	Obtains the Bean class home interface.
`getPrimaryKey()`	Returns the unique identifier of the associated Bean.
`getHandle()`	Returns an abstract handle to the EJBObject instance that can be used at a later time to reestablish a reference to the EJBObject.
`isIdentical()`	Tests whether a given EJBObject is identical to the invoked EJBObject.
`remove()`	Removes (deletes) the EJB instance and the associated EJBObject.

The EJBObject class that implements this interface is an RMI server object because it implements an RMI remote interface. Note that the Bean itself is not a remote object and is not visible over the network. When the container instantiates an EJBObject class, it initializes it with the reference to the Bean object so that it can delegate the business method calls appropriately.

Since the EJBObject must formally implement the remote interface of the Bean, container vendors can generate the EJBObject's source code at deployment time. The EJBObject is typically given a unique class name (which is not relevant to the client since the client always refers to the remote interface). The EJBObject is associated with the Bean's class as its EJBObject class.

The Enterprise Java Bean itself should not implement the remote interface because it includes the methods of the `EJBObject` interface, making it a remote interface. However, the Bean must provide implementations of the listed business methods.

Identifying Enterprise JavaBeans

A client expects that an Enterprise Java Bean has a unique identifier in order to be accessible. This unique identifier is generated in different ways for Session and Entity Beans. Whenever a Bean instance has a unique identifier associated with it, it is said to have *identity*.

Unique identifiers for Session Beans are maintained internally by the container only. Because session objects are meant to be private to only one client, they appear, from the client's view, to be anonymous. Therefore, session objects hide their identity, although the client can request a handle for the session object so it can reacquire its session at a later time.

For Entity Beans, the Bean provider must supply a unique primary key for the entity; the key must be valid within the Bean's home. The container determines Entity Bean identities by combining the home and the Bean's primary key. If two Bean instances of the same EJB class have the same primary key, they are considered identical. For an Entity Bean representing a row in a table that is uniquely identified by multiple fields, the primary key is likely a representation of all the values building the composite key for that row. It is the developer's responsibility to define a Java class that represents the primary key for an Entity Bean class. The container embeds the primary key into the EJBObject's identifier at activation time.

The home interface must always make the following method available to clients.

```
public Remote findByPrimaryKey(Object key);
```

Note that the primary key uniquely identifies the Bean instance only within its class, or home. The container is responsible for ensuring this distinction. The client can obtain the primary key of an entity at any time and can use the primary key later to reestablish a reference to the entity.

The class type of the primary key must be specified in the deployment descriptor. Bean developers can represent the primary key by any class type they prefer. The only requirement is that the class must implement the `java.io.Serializable` interface since it must be possible to pass the primary key between the client and server by value.

Testing the identity of two Bean objects should always be done by means of the `isIdentical()` method, defined in the `javax.ejb.EJBObject` interface, because the EJB specification does not define equality of two Bean instances based on the equality of their remote interfaces. Therefore, the result of performing the `object.equals()` method on an EJBObject reference is unspecified. Also, performing `object.hashCode()` on two EJBObject references representing the same EJB instance is not guaranteed to produce the same result.

The Home Interface

A client uses the home interface to locate, create, or remove (delete) instances of a specific EJB class. The home interface has a one-to-one relationship with an EJB class because it defines methods that must have a corresponding implementation in the EJB class. For every EJB class, the developer must define a distinct home interface.

However, the implementation of the home interface must be provided by the container because it involves container-specific functionality (that is, life-cycle services, etc.). The container vendor should provide the means to generate the home object implementation from the home interface at deployment time.

A client needing the use of an Enterprise Java Bean creates one through the Bean's home interface. The home interface lists one or more `create()` methods that can be used to create an instance of this Enterprise Java Bean. This home interface is not implemented by the Bean but by some other class we'll call the *home object*. This home object is instantiated within the server and made available to clients as a factory for the Enterprise Java Bean.

The client can be written in Java and can use Java RMI to access the home object and the EJBObjects or it can be written in another language, using CORBA/IIOP, provided the required server-side components are deployed in a manner that makes them accessible through CORBA interfaces.

Methods in the Home Interface

The home interface is defined as extending from the `javax.ejb.EJBHome` interface. This interface has the following methods.

```
public interface javax.ejb.EJBHome extends java.rmi.Remote {
   public EJBMetaData getEJBMetaData() throws
      RemoteException;
   public void remove(Handle handle)
      throws RemoteException,RemoveException;
   public void remove(Object primaryKey)
      throws RemoteException, RemoveException;
}
```

`getEJBMetaData()`	Obtains the Bean's metadata interface that enables the client to obtain information about the Bean's associated classes.
`remove()`	Removes (deletes) the EJBObject identified either by its handle or the Bean's primary key (two different signatures).

Since the client accesses the home object that implements the home interface on the server, it needs to be an RMI remote object, as indicated by the interface definition above (`extends java.rmi.Remote`). The client gains access to the remote home object by means of a client-side stub (a proxy object on the client).

Factory Methods

A client wanting to create a new Bean can only do so by using the home interface of the Bean's class. Let us hope the developer of the Bean has defined at least one `create()` method in the home interface for the Bean. For stateful Session Beans or Entity Beans, the developer may have defined multiple `create(...)` methods with different parameter signatures that can be used to initialize the state of the Bean object at creation time. Stateless Session Beans must provide exactly one `create()` method without any parameters to enable the container to make use of the specific characteristics of stateless Session Beans (refer to "Stateless Session Beans" on page 25 for an explanation).

These factory methods must have corresponding counterparts with matching signatures but with a slightly different method name in the Bean class in order to be called on behalf of the client.

The home interface for a Bank Account Bean might look like this.

```
public interface AccountHome extends EJBHome {
   ...
   public Account create() throws RemoteException;
   public Account create(String acctNum)
      throws RemoteException;
   ...
}
```

where `Account` is defined as:

```
public interface Account extends EJBObject { ... }
```

The Bean's class must implement the following two methods that correspond to the `create()` and `create(String acctNum)` methods in the home interface.

```
public void ejbCreate() { // create empty account... }
public void ejbCreate(String acctNum) {
    // create account and set acctNum attribute... }
```

The container vendor is responsible for creating the home object that implements the `AccountHome` interface, since only the vendor can implement the code that can act as the factory to create the Account Beans.

Finder Methods

Entity Beans usually also have finder methods that allow clients to look up existing Beans based on their identity. To access an existing Entity Bean, a client calls a finder method defined in the home interface. The name of each finder method must start with `find`, and the return type must be the Bean's remote interface (or an enumeration, see below). Note that the home interface of every Entity Bean must include the `findByPrimaryKey(<PrimaryKeyClass> primaryKey)` method.

Here is an example of two possible finder methods in the `AccountHome` home interface introduced above.

```
public interface AccountHome extends EJBHome {
    ...
    public Account findByPrimaryKey(String accountNum)
        throws RemoteException, FinderException;
    public Account findByName(String first, String last)
        throws RemoteException, FinderException;
    ...
}
```

When the client invokes one of the above methods on the home object, the container passes the invocation to the corresponding method in the Entity Bean class. The Bean class, therefore, needs to implement the following methods.

```
public class AccountEntityBean implements EntityBean {
    ...
    public Object ejbFindByPrimaryKey(String accountNum) {
```

```
// runs appropriate singleton SELECT statement
// returns primary key for selected row
}
public Object ejbFindByName(String first, String last) {
// runs appropriate singleton SELECT statement
// returns primary key for selected row
}
...
}
```

Notice that the finder methods in the home interface return a remote EJBObject reference back to the client (`Account extends EJBObject`), whereas the finder methods in the Bean return a unique identifier, or primary key object, to the container. The container will use this primary key to create a new EJBObject associated with the selected Entity Bean instance.

A good way to think of a finder method is as a database SELECT statement, where the parameters supply the dynamic SQL parameters. It is likely that a finder method may find several rows of a database table that meet the criteria specified by its arguments. In this case, the finder method must be defined to return an enumeration of primary keys instead of a single identifier object. The corresponding finder method in the home interface is defined to return an enumeration of EJBObjects.

The following code is an example of a finder method returning multiple entity references.

```
public interface AccountHome extends EJBHome {
   ...
   public Enumeration findByAccountType(String accountType)
      throws RemoteException;
   ...
}

public class AccountEntityBean implements EntityBean {
   ...
   public Enumeration ejbFindByAccountType(String
         accountType) {
   // runs appropriate SELECT statement
   // returns Enumeration of primary keys for all rows found
   }
   ...
}
```

Now that we understand the purpose of the home interface, there remains the task of the client accessing it. This task is what the next section is about.

Locating the Home Object

For a client to obtain a remote reference to a home object for a specific Enterprise JavaBean class, the client needs a location facility and some logical identification for the home object in the search facility.

Enterprise JavaBeans relies on the Java Naming and Directory Interface (JNDI) API to register and locate the home object for an Enterprise Java Bean. A reference to the home object must be registered with a naming service by the container. The EJB server will likely provide some sort of name server implementation that supports the Java JNDI API, although an external namespace could be used. Please refer to "Java Naming and Directory Interface (JNDI)" on page 117 for an in-depth description of the Java JNDI concepts.

When the deployer installs the Enterprise Java Bean into the EJB server, he or she may have the option of specifying a particular location, such as `myBank/accounting/Account`, in the naming tree for the home interface. The client must be given this fully qualified path name to locate and obtain the reference to the `Accounts` home object. Additionally, the location of the namespace and the JNDI context factory class name must be provided to the client for access to the proper naming context.

The following example illustrates a typical home object lookup scenario.

```
Context context = new InitialContext();
AccountHome accountHome =
    java.rmi.PortableRemoteObject.narrow(
        context.lookup("myBank/accounting/Accounts")
    );
```

The Complete Picture

Figure 2–4 illustrates the full picture of how to look up a specific Bean in an EJB container located on an EJB server that also provides a naming service. The steps shown in the figure must generally be performed by any client wishing to interact with an EJB instance located on a EJB server. Note that in the figure, the Naming Service is also provided by the EJB server, but it is equally possible for the Naming Service to be located on any other server accessible by the client.

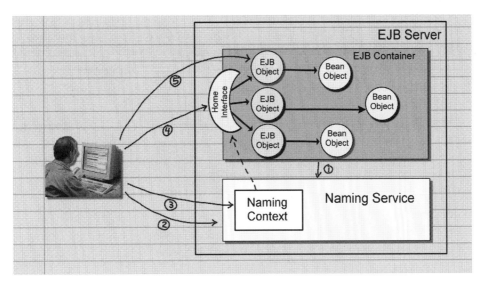

Figure 2-4 *Looking Up an EJB Object — The Full Picture*

The following steps are required for a client to look up a specific EJB object.

1. The container registers the EJB class home interface with the naming service.

2. The client contacts the naming service and obtains the naming context of the home interface by providing the appropriate context identification.

3. The client looks up the home interface referenced in the naming context by passing the fully qualified path to the context. The naming context returns a remote reference to the EJB home interface object on the server.

4. The client requests an EJBObject from the home interface by using an appropriate finder method and proper identification for the object. The home interface returns a reference to the remote EJBObject instance associated with the EJB object requested.

5. The client is now able to call a business method on the EJB object. The method call is mediated by the EJBObject instance associated to the EJB object by the container.

EJB Containers

An EJB container is an abstract system for managing EJB classes and their instances. Enterprise Java Beans of different classes can live within the same container. The container provides services, such as life-cycle management, security, and transaction coordination to the Beans. A container also provides an operation environment for its components, including operating system services such as processes or threads in which the Beans can execute, concurrency control, memory management, and so on. The container itself relies on an execution environment provided by an EJB server to provide these services to its components.

The Enterprise Java Beans gain access to the services offered by the container through the Bean interfaces defined in the EJB specification. Notice that a Bean instance never calls upon the container to execute a specific service. It is always the container that calls the Bean's hook-methods to notify an instance about certain circumstances or events. This principle is generally known as the *Hollywood Principle* ("Don't call us, we'll call you") and is the core mechanism for frameworks. There is no API available for the Bean to interact directly with the container.

A container vendor may choose to provide further interfaces to additional services implemented either in the container or in the server. Be aware that Beans using these additional services suffer from portability restrictions.

Among the services and tools a container must provide are:

- Management of critical resources, such as memory through swapping Beans to and from secondary storage (Session Beans only)

- Provision of container-managed persistence by transparently saving and loading Beans from a database (Entity Beans only)

- Availability of a home object that offers clients creation and lookup functions for Beans

- Visibility of the home object(s) in a JNDI-accessible namespace

- Life-cycle management of Beans, that is, proper creation, initialization, and destruction of Beans

- A guarantee that business methods run in the proper transaction context

- Enforcement of certain basic security services when required

- Tools for generating the implementations for the home object and the EJBObject classes

- Tools for the generation of RMI stub and skeleton classes for remote objects, such as the home object and EJBObjects

The term container should not be taken literally as a class but rather as a level of functionality and responsibility toward the components it houses. The physical manifestation of an EJB container is not defined in the Enterprise JavaBeans specification. One container vendor might provide a single physical entity, such as a multithreaded process running within one EJB server. Another vendor could implement his container as a logical entity that can be replicated and distributed across any number of systems and processes to provide better scalability.

The following sections describe in more detail some of the most important features EJB containers provide. We mainly cover the characteristics that are important for the Bean developer to understand in more depth.

Wrapping the Beans

An EJB container maintains control over client interactions with Bean instances through wrapper objects. Client applications never directly interact with an Enterprise JavaBean instance. Instead, the client application receives a remote reference to an external representation, called an EJBObject, of the Enterprise Java Bean. For every Bean created or looked up by a client, the container creates a new EJBObject instance that exposes the application-related interface of the Bean to the client but does not expose the interface that allows the EJB container to manage and control the Bean.

The EJBObject allows the EJB container to intercept operations made on the Enterprise Java Bean. Each time a client invokes a method on the EJB object, the request goes through the EJBObject instance and may be passed to the container before being delegated to the Enterprise Java Bean. By making use of this interception mechanism, the EJB container implements state management, transaction control, and security services transparently to both the client and the Enterprise Java Bean.

Relationship Between a Container and the EJBObject

Both the container and the EJBObject have distinct entry points into the Bean, giving each a unique ability to provide support for a specific service. For example, the container knows which transaction attributes apply to the methods of the Bean by reading its deployment descriptor. However, it is through the EJBObject that these business methods are invoked. The EJBObject must communicate with the container to determine in what transaction context to call the business method. Once this is determined, the EJBObject must establish this transaction context before invoking the business method.

This process indicates that there is a strong collaboration between the EJBObject and a container to implement the services required by an Enterprise Java Bean. Since container vendors provide the implementations of both the EJBObject and the container, they are free to partition this work any way they like.

Life-Cycle Management

An EJB container provides life-cycle management for each object it maintains. The container implements a factory interface for each Bean class with one or more `create()` methods so that clients can create new objects of that class.

For entity objects, the container also exposes finder methods that allow a client to locate specific Bean entities. The factory and finder interfaces are implemented by the container according to the home interface for an Enterprise JavaBean class defined by the Bean developer. Please refer to "The Home Interface" on page 34 for more details on the client's view of the home interface.

A client is usually allowed to destroy Bean instances by using the `remove()` method in either the home interface or the EJBObject interface of the appropriate Enterprise Java Bean.

Finding Entity Beans

When the client invokes a finder method on the home object, the container either creates a new Entity Bean instance (that has no valid content yet) or reuses a privately held anonymous Bean object of the appropriate class to perform the request. The container transfers the `find...()` method call to the appropriate `ejbFind...()` method for the Bean to execute the logic of finding the entities identified by the parameters the client passed to the finder method. Regardless of the implementation of the finder method, its implementation in the Bean must always return to the container just the primary key of the underlying entity data (that is, a row in a database table). If multiple entities meet the search criteria, then multiple primary keys are returned to the container.

When a finder method returns a primary key to the container, the container first checks to see if an EJBObject with that primary key already exists. If so, the container does not create a new EJBObject but returns the reference to the existing EJBObject to the client. This ensures that there is only one EJBObject instance for each specific entity and that all clients share the same object. If the container does not already hold a corresponding EJBObject, it instantiates a new one (or multiple ones if more than one key has been returned by the finder method) and initializes it with the primary keys of the underlying entities. The container then has the option of immediately instantiating the Entity Bean instance(s) associated with the EJBObject(s) or postponing this action to a later time, that is, the first time a method call is issued on a new Bean, thus conserving memory resources.

Maintaining Persistence

The EJB container manages the state of its Bean instances differently for Session and Entity Beans. *State* refers to the data contained within a Bean instance, that is, the conversational state of a Session Bean object or the data of an Entity Bean instance.

Session Bean state is usually transient, and the container does not need to provide any means to make it automatically persistent. In some cases, session object state pertains only to the execution of a single method invocation, while in other cases, the state must be maintained across multiple method invocations. The latter case usually involves transaction coordination.

Entity Beans usually represent a business entity in a datastore, and their state must persist over container downtimes or crashes. Hence, the container is required to provide the means for automatic, container-managed persistence, although Bean developers may choose to implement their own persistence within the Bean, thus applying the Bean-managed persistence model. Both models usually involve transaction coordination through the container.

For a container to offer container-managed persistence, the required functionality is usually implemented in the container at Bean deployment time. This implementation requires the support of vendor tools capable of mapping the persistent fields of an Enterprise Java Bean to the underlying datastore. The containers rely on the EJB server to provide the appropriate drivers or backend connections.

Because of the considerable difference in the handling of the persistence requirements for Entity Beans, as opposed to Session Beans, a container provider may deliver different container implementations for each type of Bean. Please refer to "Persistence" on page 71 for a detailed introduction to persistence handling.

Controlling Transactions

One of the key features of the EJB architecture is support for distributed transactions. The container implements the transaction API toward the Beans. The Enterprise server must implement the necessary low-level transaction protocols for the container to use. An EJB container must support both implicit and explicit transaction management to both Session and Entity Beans.

Implicit transaction management denotes that the container is transparently using transaction management in accordance with the transaction attributes provided in the deployment descriptor of the Bean. The transaction attributes and isolation levels can be defined either for the entire Bean or individually for each of the Bean's methods.

If a Bean is to explicitly demarcate the transaction boundaries in its methods, a developer can use the Java Transaction Interface (JTA) to programmatically interact with the underlying transaction service. The container provides access to the `javax.jts.UserTransaction` interface through the `EJBContext` interface, which is implemented by the `SessionContext` and `EntityContext` that the container provides to each session and entity object, respectively.

Please refer to "Transaction Management" on page 77 for a detailed introduction to EJB transaction handling.

Serializing Method Calls

The container is responsible for serializing all method calls on Beans regardless of whether they are issued by a client or by the container itself. This frees the Bean developer from complex issues, such as making the Bean's methods reentrant, but it has some implications with regard to loopback calls. Please refer to "Serialization of Method Calls" on page 26 and to "Synchronizing Method Concurrency" on page 27 for details.

Naming

Enterprise JavaBeans clients rely on the Java Naming and Directory Interface (JNDI) API to locate the home interfaces for a specific Enterprise JavaBean class. It is the container's responsibility to make the Bean's home interfaces available to clients by registering the Bean with a naming service capable of providing a JNDI-conforming API to the client.

The client also needs some information as to which naming context and under which path the home interface can be found. Normally, this information is provided to the container by means of a deployment descriptor property. This information must also be provided to the client.

Resource Management

For a container to support a large number of Beans efficiently, it needs certain means to manage its working set in an effective way. The term *working set* denotes the set of Beans a container needs to keep actively running in memory at any time. The specification defines an activation and deactivation mechanism that can be used by the container to swap out Beans from memory to secondary storage, thus freeing memory for other Beans that need to be activated. The implementation of the mechanism is not defined by the specification, leaving vendors free to implement anything from basic to very sophisticated algorithms. Although the mechanism is totally transparent to the client, a Bean may have to implement certain methods to manage its resources in a controlled manner.

Bean instances that hold critical resources, such as database connections, open files, or network communication sockets, should free these resources when the container decides to passivate the Bean. To free resources, instances must implement the necessary functionality in the `ejbPassivate()` method, which is called by the container immediately before swapping out the Bean. The container invokes the `ejbActivate()` method to notify passivated Beans before any of their business methods are called as a result of a client issuing a business method call. In there, the Bean should implement the code to reacquire the necessary resources. If the Bean does not use resources that must be released prior to passivation or reset on activation, then these methods can be left empty.

If the Bean is currently in a transaction, it will not be passivated. It is more efficient to leave the Bean in memory since transactions normally complete within a fairly short period of time.

A container can use any appropriate mechanism to store the Bean persistently while it is in the passivated state. The most likely means of doing such storage is serialization of the Bean. That's why the Bean and all its fields should be serializable. The Bean developer also should avoid using transient fields in the Bean because they will not be restored automatically at Bean activation time. If the developer still decides to use transient fields, it is his responsibility to restore these fields in the `ejbActivate()` methods to some meaningful value.

Activation and Passivation of Entity Beans

From a Bean's point of view, activation and passivation work in a similar fashion to Session Beans. However, Entity Beans can be considered stateless when they are not involved in a transaction because their state is always synchronized with the underlying datastore after a transaction has completed.

This would allow the container to just destroy the Entity Bean instances instead of swapping them out. However, since the container will need anonymous Entity Beans to invoke finder methods (refer to "Finding Entity Beans" on page 42 for an explanation), the container may likely passivate Entity Beans into a private in-memory pool for this purpose. Once the Entity Bean instance is passivated, it no longer has an identity (that is, a primary key association), although its EJBObject instance remains allocated and valid all the time.

The container can also use this in-memory pool for reallocation of Entity Beans when a business method is requested on an EJBObject that currently has no corresponding Entity Bean associated. Remember that when a Bean is in this pool, it has no identity and can be reused by any other EJBObject. Before the call is routed to the Bean instance, its state is synchronized with the underlying entity in the datastore. The container can even implement a policy that does not maintain any active Entity Beans except the ones on which a business method is currently executed or the ones involved in a transaction.

Bean Runtime Context Information

All Bean containers must provide their Bean instances with context information to give the objects access to the context maintained by the container.

Although two context interfaces are defined for Entity and Session Beans, most of the methods defined in the two interfaces have the same signature and provide the same functionality. The `EntityContext` and `SessionContext` interfaces both derive from the `EJBContext` interface, whose methods are briefly described below.

`getEJBHome()`	Returns the instance's home object.
`getEnvironment()`	Returns the environment properties list with which the Bean was deployed.
`getCallerIdentity()`	Returns the security identity of the current invoker of the Bean's EJBObject instance.
`setRollbackOnly()`	Allows the instance to mark the current transaction such that the outcome is forced to roll back.
`getRollbackOnly()`	Tests whether the transaction outcome has been marked for rollback.
`isCallerInRole()`	Tests whether the Bean's caller has a particular role.
`getUserTransaction()`	Returns the `javax.jts.UserTransaction` interface that the Bean can use for explicit transaction demarcation.

The `EntityContext` interface adds the following methods to the context for Entity Beans.

`getEJBObject()`	Returns the EJBObject for the instance.
`getPrimaryKey()`	Obtains the instance's primary key.

The `SessionContext` interface adds only the method `getEJBObject()`, which returns the Bean's EJBObject instance.

The EJB Server Environment

This section focuses on the infrastructure of an EJB environment, called the Enterprise JavaBeans Execution System, or, in short, the EJB server. It broadly explains the set of services that vendors must provide to support the execution of Enterprise Java Beans.

An Enterprise JavaBeans server must basically support the deployment, execution, and management of Enterprise Java Beans. It makes up the base of the component execution system and provides the runtime platform for one or more EJB containers and their Enterprise Java Beans inside.

Difference Between an EJB Container and a Server

Currently, there is no interface, or even a sharp line, defining the difference between a container and an EJB server. The EJB specification (version 1.0) does not distinctly divide the EJB execution system responsibilities between an EJB container and an EJB server. This division has been deferred to a future release of the specification. So, it is up to the vendors to freely choose an implementation model that fulfills the interfaces to the Enterprise Java Beans and provides all required services. Also, the exact nature of process management, thread-pooling, concurrency control, and resource management is not defined within the scope of the EJB specification. Individual vendors can differentiate their products by the simplicity or sophistication of the services. Software vendors might elect to develop new component execution systems specifically to support Enterprise Java Beans. However, it is more likely that vendors will adapt their existing products to support EJBs. In most circumstances, a single vendor provides both an EJB server and an associated EJB container, although the specification allows the separation of these services.

An EJB server can host one or multiple EJB containers. The containers are transparent to the client; there is no client API to manipulate the container, and there is no way for a client to tell in which container an Enterprise Java Bean is installed. Given these circumstances, let's define the terms for server and container.

- **EJB server** — A specific, usually physical, system or product that provides the execution services for one or more EJB containers. Additionally, an EJB Server provides the necessary drivers or interfaces to access remote or local systems providing services for distributed transactions, persistence, and naming.

- **EJB container** — An abstract system that provides the required interfaces and services for Enterprise Java Beans as defined by the EJB specification. An EJB container relies on the runtime environment and service accessors of an EJB server to fulfill its responsibilities.

EJB Server Responsibilities

EJB servers provide the base of the Enterprise JavaBeans execution systems, so they must provide a standard set of services to support Enterprise Java Beans. Enterprise Java Beans are transactional. Therefore, an EJB server must provide access to a distributed transaction management service. Entity Beans require persistence, so the server must provide some means of datastore access or backend system connection. The EJB server must also provide a container for the Enterprise Java Beans that implement the management and control services for the Enterprise JavaBeans classes.

Let's look at some of these responsibilities in more detail.

Providing a Container Runtime Environment

This is the most basic requirement an EJB server must fulfill — it must be able to support one or more EJB containers. To do this, a server must provide the following basic services and more.

- **Multithreading** — Each method call to an EJB can run in its own thread.

- **Efficient memory management** — Although a container will try to minimize Bean creation and destruction by providing pools, Java requires efficient memory management for the Java virtual machine.

- **Exception handling** — It is the container's responsibility to handle exceptions and delegate them to the Enterprise Java Beans where necessary.

Providing Access to a Distributed Transaction System

The EJB server must either provide access to a remote transaction system or directly implement such a service. The transaction service must provide flat (non-nested) transactions modeled after the OMG Object Transactional Service 1.1 (OTS). The transaction system must support the functionality for user transactions as defined in the Java Transaction API (JTA). This is the only transaction interface a container must provide to its Beans.

Providing Access to a Datastore

An EJB server must (optionally) provide access to a datastore that supports the JDBC interface. The datastore can be a relational database or a backend application that provides for persistent storage of Entity Bean status.

In the EJB specification 1.0, this service is optional because container support for Entity Beans is an optional feature. However, container support for Entity Beans will become mandatory in version 2.0.

Providing Access to a Naming Service

A container must be able to register the home interfaces with a JNDI-compliant naming service so that clients can gain access to the home interface and, through it, to the Beans.

The EJB server is not required to run such a naming service locally, but it needs to provide access to a naming service within a network domain that can be reached by all clients. Generally, some JNDI-compliant naming service must be available within reach of both the server and the clients.

Protocol Support

To provide for broad interoperability with clients and other EJB servers, the runtime environment should support the following TCP/IP-based protocols.

- **JRMP** — The native RMI protocol. Mandatory.

- **IIOP** — The CORBA protocol for interoperability with Java and non-Java systems. IIOP interoperability is mandatory only if the EJB environment supports the EJB-to-CORBA mapping.

- **HTTP** — An optional protocol used if the server provides HTML services (this is not part of the EJB specification).

Tools Support

This section briefly touches on the tools a container or EJB server provider should deliver.

EJB Deployment Tools

Deployment tools must be provided by the container vendor because they provide functionality that is specific for a certain type of container.

- **Tools to read EJB Jar files.** The container must include tools that support deployment of Enterprise JavaBeans packaged in the EJB Jar file format. The tools must discover all the Enterprise Java Beans that are in the Jar file by reading the EJB Jar manifest file and must provide the following functionality for each Bean found.

  - Read the information contained in the Bean's deployment descriptor.

  - Generate the container-specific classes for the EJBObject and the home interface.

  - Generate the classes for stubs and skeletons used by the underlying distributed objects protocol.

  - Make the Enterprise JavaBeans home interface available in JNDI so clients can find and access the Enterprise Java Beans.

  - Make the Enterprise Java Bean's environment properties available to the Bean instances at runtime.

- **Tools to manage deployment descriptor attributes.** The EJB container may provide tools that allow the EJB deployer to modify the information imported from the Enterprise JavaBean's deployment descriptor. In certain scenarios, the tools may restrict the deployer from changing some or all deployment descriptor attributes. However, the EJB specification does not specify which attributes can or cannot be changed at deployment time.

- **Tools to customize business logic.** The EJB container may provide tools that allow the EJB deployer to customize business logic of the deployed Enterprise Java Beans. For example, the tools may allow the deployer to write *wrapper* functions for the business methods. To allow maximum freedom for the tool vendors, the EJB specification does not architect the customization.

- **Tools for container-managed persistence.** The EJB containers that support container-managed persistence should provide tools that allow the deployer to map the container-managed fields to an enterprise's existing data source or application system. These tools are typically specific to the data source or application system.

Runtime Management Tools

The container should provide tools that allow runtime management and monitoring of the Enterprise Java Beans running in the container.

Evolution Management Tools

The container should provide tools that allow the deployer and system administrator to manage evolution of the Enterprise JavaBeans implementation. The tools should make it possible, for example, to upgrade the business logic implemented by an Enterprise Java Bean by installing a new version of the Enterprise JavaBean class.

Chapter **3**

Distribution
Support
and Services

▼ OVERVIEW

▼ CLIENT/SERVER COMMUNICATION

Enterprise JavaBeans are server-side applications that interoperate with remote clients, and perhaps other servers, to provide a given application processing function. The client could be a pure Java client application (for example, Java Bean) or some non-Java object or application on the network, while a server could be another EJB server or some legacy system. Interoperation with different types of clients and servers over the network means that an EJB server must provide support for multiple forms of distribution.

Distribution is a generic reference for distributed computing models, such as client-server, peer-to-peer, and other forms of distributed computing including Enterprise JavaBeans. By definition, Enterprise JavaBeans is a component architecture for the development and deployment of cross-platform, distributed server components that are capable of supporting distributed transactional applications.

Since the Enterprise JavaBeans specification allows for any kind of client and does not mandate any particular remote object protocol, an EJB server may implement

51

several forms of distribution. For instance, client access to an Enterprise Java Bean, using a servlet and the HTTP (Hypertext Transfer Protocol), could be one form of distribution. In this case, the client (most likely a Web browser) makes a request through HTTP that is received by a Web server. The Web server forwards the request to the servlet, which gains access to the Enterprise JavaBean object through the EJB object and home interfaces. Other forms of distribution are also possible and may require the EJB server environment to support a variety of protocols and services.

This chapter focuses on the distribution support outlined in the Enterprise Java-Beans specification for client access to an Enterprise JavaBeans object. A discussion of the three-tier application architecture is also provided, along with a discussion of services that are likely to be offered by an EJB server vendor for support of Enterprise JavaBeans.

Overview

The Enterprise JavaBeans model is based on a distributed computing architecture where any number of tiers of application logic and business services are separated into components that communicate with each other across a network. In its most basic form, the model can be depicted as a logical, three-tier computing model with a separation of processing into client, application, and data. A typical three-tier architecture consists of the following elements.

- A client tier containing logic related to the presentation of information and requests to applications through a workstation.

- Web application servers that provide standard interfaces, protocols, and services for support of business application processing. A representative infrastructure may include a Web server and an EJB server with services for TCP/IP, HTTP, directory, and security.

- Resource managers that provide data storage and access to other transaction systems through a set of connectors.

The three-tier distributing computing model is represented in Figure 3–1.

Distribution Through RMI

The standard mechanism for client communication with an Enterprise Java Bean is through the Java Remote Method Invocation (RMI) API. RMI extends the pure Java object model to the network and makes the location of the server transparent to the client. It enables objects in one Java virtual machine (for example, the client machine) to seamlessly invoke methods on objects in another Java virtual

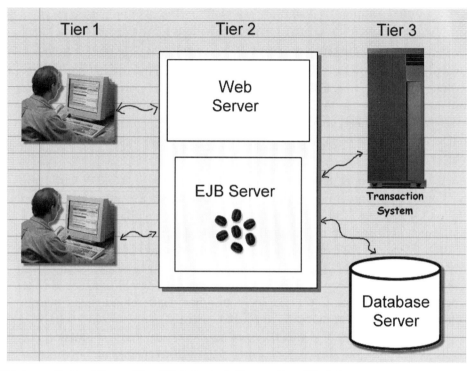

Figure 3-1 *Three-Tier Distributed Computing Model*

machine (for example, the server), regardless of where each machine resides in the network.

RMI is flexible and extensible with the ability to use multiple transport or communication protocols, such as Java Remote Messaging Protocol (JRMP) and Internet Inter-ORB Protocol (IIOP). The use of either protocol is transparent to the Enterprise JavaBean developer and is an implementation concern only for the EJB server or container provider. When the EJB is deployed in a container, the container provides or generates two implementations: the Bean's home interface and the Bean's remote interface. The interfaces between a client and the container are detailed in "The Client's View of an EJB" on page 31.

JRMP is the native protocol for RMI allowing Java client objects to access Enterprise JavaBean objects. This capability is referred to as *RMI over JRMP*. Java client objects may also use IIOP, the industry-standard communications protocol for CORBA, for access to Enterprise JavaBeans objects. The implementation of RMI over IIOP combines the advantages of the Java RMI interface for distributed systems programming with the Object Management Group's CORBA architecture for distributed computing. A significant benefit of RMI over IIOP is that it enables the interoperability of Enterprise Java Beans with non-Java clients and servers.

Protocols other than JRMP and IIOP, such as HTTP, are not addressed by the Enterprise JavaBeans Release 1 specification. Since HTTP is the standard protocol for Internet access, most EJB server vendors will probably provide an infrastructure that enables access to Enterprise Java Beans from a Web-based client, such as a Web browser. A likely model or implementation will include Web applications that leverage Web servers, Web clients (such as Web browsers), and standard Internet protocols.

To ensure the interoperability of Enterprise Java Beans with CORBA-based implementations from numerous vendors, Sun has developed a standard mapping of EJB to CORBA. The EJB-to-CORBA mapping includes the Mapping of Distribution, which defines the relationship between an Enterprise Java Bean and a CORBA object and the mapping of Java RMI remote interfaces to the OMG's Interface Definition Language (IDL). IDL is a key feature of CORBA that enables objects to interact regardless of the language they're written in, such as the Java programming language, C, C++, COBOL, or others. Each language that supports CORBA has its own IDL mapping, including Java IDL, which supports the mapping of Java to CORBA. The Java IDL provides an Object Request Broker (ORB) that enables communication between objects. The ORB is nothing more than a class library that enables low-level communication between Java IDL applications and other CORBA-compliant applications.

Client/Server Communication

Any relationship between distributed objects has two sides: the client and the server. The server provides a remote interface, and the client calls a remote interface. These relationships are common to most distributed object standards, including object models for Java and CORBA. In this context, the terms *client* and *server* define object-level rather than application-level interaction. For instance, any application could be a server for some objects and a client of others. In fact, a single object could be the client of an interface provided by a remote object and, at the same time, implement an interface to be called remotely by other objects.

On the client side, the application includes a reference for the remote object. The object reference has a stub method, which is a stand-in or proxy for the method being called remotely. The stub is actually wired into the ORB, so that calling it invokes the ORB's connection capabilities, which forward the invocation to the server.

On the server side, the ORB uses skeleton code to translate the remote invocation into a method call on the local object. The skeleton translates the call and any parameters to their implementation-specific format and calls the method being invoked. When the method returns, the skeleton code transforms results or errors and sends them back to the client through the ORBs.

Between the ORBs, communication proceeds by means of a shared protocol, IIOP — the Internet Inter-ORB Protocol. IIOP, which is based on the standard TCP/IP internet protocol, defines how CORBA-compliant ORBs pass information back and forth. Like CORBA and IDL, the IIOP standard is defined by OMG, the Object Management Group.

In addition to these simple distributed object capabilities, CORBA-compliant ORBs can provide a number of optional services defined by the OMG. These include services for looking up objects by name, maintaining persistent objects, supporting transaction processing, enabling messaging, and many other capabilities useful in today's distributed, multitiered computing environments. Several Java ORBs from third-party vendors support some or all of these additional capabilities. The ORB provided with Java IDL supports one optional service, the capability to locate objects by name.

The Java Remote Method Protocol (JRMP) is the native protocol providing support for all functions within the RMI API. RMI can also use the Internet InterORB Protocol. IIOP supports almost all functions within RMI. The implementation of RMI over IIOP is a standard extension to the Java Development Kit (JDK 1.1.6) and supports almost all functions within RMI.

This model is based on an *n*-tier distributed computing architecture, where any number of tiers of application logic and business services are separated into components that communicate with each other across a network. In its most basic form, this architecture can be depicted as a logical three-tier computing model, meaning that there is a logical, but not necessarily physical, separation of functions. The wide variety of client support requires a variety of communication protocols.

Enterprise JavaBeans servers typically support three types of clients. A client, in this context, is end-user equipment, such as a workstation or personal computer, a network computer, laptop, or smaller network device, or a program in another server acting like a client. The three types of clients are listed below.

1. Clients that contain a Java environment. These clients can communicate with an EJB server by any of the following techniques.

    - Issuing native Java RMI calls over JRMP.

    - Issuing Java RMI calls over CORBA IIOP to the ORB; every EJB server provides support for an ORB. RMI over IIOP will be a standard part of every JDK beginning with JDK 1.1.6; it is based on the mapping of distribution as defined by the EJB-to-CORBA mapping specification.

- Creating standard CORBA method calls, using Java IDL to develop the appropriate stubs and skeletons, which then communicate over IIOP.

- Using GET/POST requests over HTTP to the Web server (HTTP daemon). Every EJB server environment should provide access to a Web server.

2. Clients supporting CORBA IIOP, including programs written in C and C++, using an IDL compiler and tools to generate communications that conform to the 1998 Java-to-IDL mapping (mentioned above).

3. Clients that include an industry-standard Web browser and can, therefore, use uniform resource locators (URLs) to communicate with a Web server that is accessible by the EJB server.

Figure 3–2 illustrates several ways to achieve client/server interoperability in a Java environment. In the figure, a user at a Java client platform is using the client to communicate with application code on an application server. Note that there are two major styles of communication. In one case, someone is using a Web browser to communicate with the server through the Hypertext Transfer Protocol (HTTP). HTTP is the original transport protocol for the World Wide Web. The Web browser has Hypertext Markup Language (HTML) support and communicates with an application running on the server either through the Web server with an HTML document at the server or through the Internet Common Gateway Interface (CGI). If the application is set up appropriately, it can retrieve data from a database server and return the data to the applet through the HTTP-CGI mechanism. Applications written to work with CGI are often written in a scripting language, such as the Practical Extraction and Reporting Language (PERL) or a UNIX shell script, but such applications can also be written in C or C++.

Figure 3–2 also illustrates a recent alternative to CGI, called the Java servlet. Servlets run in a Java environment on the server and are somewhat analogous to applets running on a client. Like CGI applications, servlets can access and return data through HTTP, but servlets also benefit from the portability and security characteristics of the Java environment. As is illustrated in the figure, servlets can access Enterprise Java Beans as well as Java Beans.

As Figure 3–2 illustrates, a user can also invoke a Java applet or application on the client to provide an object-oriented style of communication with the application server code. The applet in the client contains a stub; that is, the applet communicates with a remote JavaBeans function on the server through one of two object-oriented APIs: the interface definition language (IDL) of CORBA or the remote

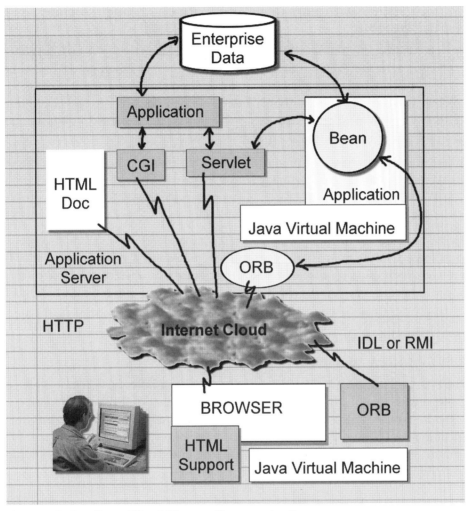

Figure 3-2 *Java Client/Server Communications*

method invocation (RMI) of Java. CORBA IDL uses a standard protocol, the Internet Inter-Orb Protocol (IIOP), whereas RMI typically uses the Java Remote Method Protocol (JRMP) or IIOP. RMI over IIOP is the preferred method when doing distributed programming in Java, whether the target object is written in Java or in another language such as C++. These protocols allow client applets and applications to invoke, through the an Object Request Broker (ORB), server functionality as if it were local. This object-oriented style of communication is used between servers as well as between servers and clients.

Interoperability with Pure Java Applications Through Remote Method Invocation

Remote Method Invocation (RMI) is a set of Java services that were developed by JavaSoft to allow applications or applets running in a Java environment to invoke methods that are provided by objects running remotely in Java applications or applets. RMI could be used for both client-to-server and server-to-server communications among Java applications or applets. RMI is a scheme for pure Java invocation of remote services (methods).

In the Java distributed object model, a remote object is one whose methods can be invoked from another Java virtual machine, potentially on a different host. An object of this type is described by one or more remote interfaces, which are Java interfaces that declare the methods of the remote object.

RMI is the action of invoking a method of a remote interface on a remote object. Most importantly, a method invocation on a remote object has the same syntax as a method invocation on a local object. RMI applications often comprise two separate programs: a server and a client. A typical server application creates a number of remote objects and makes references to those remote objects.

Interoperability with Non-Java Applications

EJB-to-CORBA Mapping

The EJB specification provides a standard mapping of Enterprise JavaBeans to CORBA with an aim to define interoperability such that CORBA-based implementations of the specification can interoperate over a network. The specification encompasses EJB-to-CORBA mapping, mapping of distribution, mapping of naming, mapping of transactions, and mapping of security. It also defines interoperability for the following scenarios.

- A CORBA client, written in any CORBA-supported language, can access Enterprise Java Beans deployed in a CORBA-based EJB server.

- A client program can mix calls to CORBA and EJB objects within a transaction.

- A transaction can span multiple EJB objects that are located on multiple CORBA-based EJB servers.

The above scenarios imply that there are two types of COBRA clients.

1.   A Java client that uses EJB APIs. The Java client uses JNDI to locate objects, uses Java RMI over IIOP to invoke remote methods, and exposes an interface to define transaction scope.

2. A CORBA client that uses any language that provides bindings of the CORBA IDL. The CORBA client uses COS Naming to locate objects, CORBA IDL to invoke remote methods, and OTS to define transaction scope.

A comprehensive explanation of this mapping can be found in *Sun Microsystems Enterprise JavaBeans to CORBA Mapping* specification. This specification is a standard mapping of the Enterprise JavaBeans 1.0 architecture to CORBA.

Drivers or Connectors

Drivers, or connectors, make it possible for an Enterprise Java Bean to interoperate with a non-EJB server.

There are no industry standards for providing access to backend systems, although Enterprise JavaBeans will provide a standard way to encapsulate the required services as objects.

The bulk of today's critical data and application programs reside on and use existing enterprise systems. Therefore, a fundamental requirement for almost any EJB server is to preserve and leverage this data and these systems without extensive modifications.

Chapter **4**

Security

▼ SECURITY FEATURES OF THE JAVA
   LANGUAGE

▼ JAVA VM SECURITY FEATURES

▼ ENTERPRISE JAVABEANS SECURITY

▼ SECURITY AND SERIALIZATION OBJECTS

▼ SECURITY OUTSIDE THE JAVA
   ENVIRONMENT

▼ SUMMARY

Security of computer systems is high on everyone's agenda. Whenever there is a security breakthrough or a hack, the story is reported in every computer magazine and often in the public news. Thanks to this publicity and exposure, everyone is aware of the impact hackers and viruses can have on a system or an organization. Any computer connected to a network is open to attack. Any user downloading or sharing software is vulnerable to viruses. Making a system secure requires a number of measures, including security processes, physical security, and logical security. So, let's look at what Java does to secure systems.

Java, from its inception, has provided a powerful set of security features to allow systems to be logically secure. Let us consider the exposures of a Java system. Figure 4–1 shows the elements of a total system.

As Figure 4–1 shows, a wide range of client systems could be accessing the services provided by an Enterprise JavaBeans server. There could be employees of a partner company using browsers to place orders and to check order status.

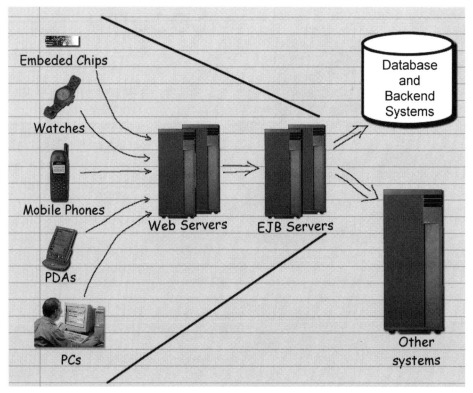

Figure 4–1   *The Elements of a Java System*

Business managers with PDAs and mobile phones could be making important business decisions regarding manufacturing plans. Java-based watches could be providing live information regarding the status of manufacturing processes. Drilling machines could be receiving new drilling sequences from embedded Java chips. Any of these client devices could be used to introduce a virus into the system, to steal vital or sensitive information or to damage or destroy a system. The Enterprise JavaBeans will be the gateway to the heart of all systems — the code databases. As such, the overall system design must include mechanisms to secure access to the Enterprise Java Beans.

All client systems based on Java can take advantage of the built-in Java security features shown in Figure 4–2.

The Enterprise JavaBeans architecture builds on all the underlying Java security features. Let's look in more detail now at the Java security building blocks, starting with the lowest level: the Java language.

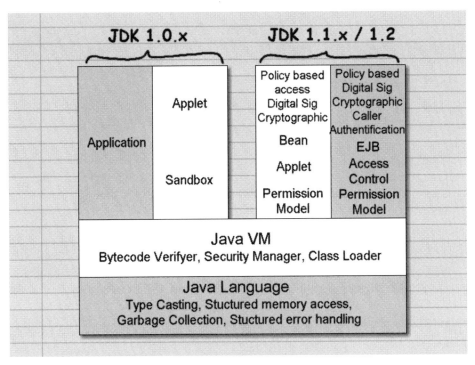

Figure 4-2 *Overall Java Security Model*

Security Features of the Java Language

Java language itself provides a number of key security features.

- Strong type casting to ensure that only like or valid references are made.

- Structured memory access with no pointer-based access or arithmetic.

- Automatic garbage collection — a Java program cannot explicitly free allocated memory and keep a dangling reference to that memory.

- Array bounds checking to stop programs from corrupting code and data outside the defined arrays.

- Checking for null references to stop stray access to data.

- Structured error handling, that is, forcing programs to handle errors correctly and not leaving security holes.

These features ensure that many accidental problems do not occur and, more importantly, that holes are not open for hackers and virus writers to exploit. Besides making systems secure, these features also make programs more robust.

Java VM Security Features

First, the Java virtual machine (VM) implements the security features of the Java language. In addition to these, the Java VM provides the following features.

- **The bytecode verifier.** The bytecode verifier is the first level of defense. All Java source programs are compiled to create platform-independent byte-codes. Before this bytecode is executed, the verifier checks that it has not been tampered with and that the code does not violate access restrictions and adheres to Java's tight type checking.

- **The class loader.** The second level of defense is the applet class loader. It controls when and how applets can add classes to the Java environment. Typically, the environment will have many class loaders active, each with its own namespace. Namespaces keep classes originating from different sources separate to ensure that they do not interfere with each other.

- **The security manager.** The third level of defense is the security manager, which limits the ways in which classes can use accessible interfaces. The security manager performs runtime checks and can veto any potentially dangerous operations by creating a security exception. The security manager will take into account a number of factors, such as the class loader that loaded the class and the source of the class (for example, built-in versus downloaded over the Internet).

JDK 1.0.x Security

The JDK 1.0.x security was essentially an on or off mechanism.

The Java applications designer/developer conformed to the security requirements of the Java language and the Java virtual machine. Beyond this, the Java code could have been an application with no security restrictions other than those explicitly written by the developer.

Applets, on the other hand, were totally constrained. Users downloading code over the network needed to be confident that the code would not damage their system. The Java security model constrained Java applets to within the boundaries of the Sandbox. The Sandbox stopped the applet from the following actions.

- Reading from or writing to a local disk

- Making connections to the host from which the applet came

- Creating a new process

- Loading a new dynamic library and calling a native method

By stopping the code from carrying out these kinds of actions, the Java security model stopped untrusted code from corrupting a system. The Sandbox was implemented by a combination of the Java VM's bytecode verifier, class loader, and the security manager.

JDK 1.1.x Security

JDK 1.1.x brought a number of significant enhancements to Java security: key management for both private and public keys and the capability to create and validate message digests and digital signatures.

These enhancements are provided by a new architecture: Java Cryptography Architecture (JCA) and the Java Cryptography Extension (JCE). The JCA provides the basic cryptographic facilities, and the JCE extends these to provide encryption and key exchange. These architectures provide implementation independence and interoperability. Also, the algorithms used are independent of the applications and are extensible. The JCA and JCE are implemented by four new groups of classes.

- Engine class — The generic class in the Java security that creates implementations of cryptographic algorithms. This class provides the core interface to the specific algorithms implemented.

- Signature class — An engine class that implements the algorithms used for creating and verifying the signature algorithms, such as DSA and RSA with MD5. This class creates an associated signature from any input. Given a signature, the class can verify whether or not the signature is authentic.

- MessageDigest class — Another engine class; it provides, creates, and verifies a message digest. The digests are unique to the data provided to the class and essentially provide a digital fingerprint of the data.

- Key interface — Defines all the functionality shared by all key objects. It defines the three main functions that keys provide: the algorithm; the encoding form, for example, X.509 or PKCS#8; and the format that is the name for this encoded key.

  Two classes are part of the interface. The KeyPair class is the holder for the pair of keys (that is, the private key and public key). The engine class that generates pairs of private and public keys is the KeyPairGenerator.

These enhancements allow the creation of signed applets that can be trusted and that can have unconstrained access to resources. In addition, these architectures allow the creation of a greater level of security within applications.

JDK 1.2 Security

The JDK 1.2 introduces two new concepts.

- Permissions and policies

- Domain-based security

In addition to these new concepts, JDK 1.2 introduced support for X.509 v3 certificates and improved the security tools.

The new concepts mean that all Java code has to be granted permission to access resources. This applies to applications, applets, servlets, Java Beans, and Enterprise Java Beans. So, if the instance does not have the correct permissions, it has to remain within the Sandbox. With the right permissions, it can have open access to all the resources.

The use of policies and permissions provides granular access to a wide range of resources.

- Files or directories — either read and/or write

- Connections to hosts or ports

- Methods of a class — either invoke or destroy

- Access to an Enterprise Java Bean

For code to access a resource, explicit access needs to be granted; the default is no access.

Enterprise JavaBeans Security

So far, we have explored, at a high level, the security facilities of the Java environment. The Enterprise Java Beans bring with them a different set of security requirements. These requirements are not new; they are the same requirements we now expect from transaction monitors. In summary, these are:

- Identifying and authenticating the caller

- Managing access to resources according to security policy definitions

67

To support these requirements, the Enterprise JavaBeans architecture builds on the existing Java security facilities to do the following.

- Obtain the identity of the calling client and the security role of the caller.

- Define the level of access for individual methods or Beans.

- Define the identity the Bean should assume when making calls to other resources (for example, databases or remote systems). The Bean can assume the identity of the client, the server system, or another user.

In addition to these Java security facilities, Enterprise Java Beans need to use additional security facilities.

- Encryption of client messages, using HTTPS

- Specific facilities of additional resources accessed by the Bean, for example, databases, CORBA systems, or legacy systems

The combination of all the security facilities discussed in this section allows an Enterprise Java Bean to have the security capabilities that any enterprise implementation will demand.

Security and Serialization Objects

Serialization is the process of saving an object to disk and later restoring it. The object is then outside the secure confines of the Java environment. There is a potential exposure here, in that the serialized object may be tampered with prior to restoration, thus inserting viruses into the object.

The serialization model includes a base set of features to limit this exposure.

- Only those objects that have been explicitly coded as serializable or externalizable can be serialized. This feature can be limited to specific fields and classes, thus limiting the exposure to only that specific area.

- Objects cannot be overwritten by a deserialization process. The deserialization process only creates new objects.

- Any code loaded during, or by, deserialization is protected by the Java security discussed so far.

- Fields or objects that should not be written out as part of a serialization request can be declared as transient. For example, file handles that will be specific to a particular instance should be declared as transient.

- Class-specific serialization methods can be written that perform additional checks to ensure the deserialized object has not been changed, for example, if there were particular rules for the relationship of data items.

- The serialized object can be encrypted as it is produced. There are two options for how this encryption can be achieved. The first option is to use class-specific serialization/deserialization methods that implement encryption. The second is to use a different stream or filter that implements the encryption.

Security Outside the Java Environment

Finally, not all the systems will be within the Java environment. The Java systems will connect to existing server systems. Other non-Java systems will be accessing Java services. It is outside the scope of this book to look at all the security techniques that can be deployed for these cases. However, the following techniques are commonly used.

- **Network-level security or IPSEC** — This is a rather heavy-handed approach to security in that all the IP messages are encrypted. It has a high cost associated with it and protects from important threats, such as listening to messages, spoofing (or emulating a server), and flooding (that is, overloading a server with requests).

- **SSL, or Secure Sockets Layer** — This provides the option of securing a communications session or not. However, once the session is open, all the traffic between the two partners is encrypted.

- **HTTPS, or Secure HTTP** — This is the technique to encrypt the HTTP or Web requests and responses. This approach allows the applications to selectively secure individual requests or groups of requests.

- **Authentication and passwords** — This is one of the most commonly used and well-understood approaches to securing access to a system. The one-time password, a recent technique, is very effective in securing access to systems. In this approach, a user needing to access a system is provided with a small device that provides a unique password for the individual user to use at that time. The server checks that the password is correct before allowing access. If someone were to find the password and try to use it, the server would reject the attempt because it would be expecting a different code.

Summary

Security is a complex topic that must not be ignored or overlooked. We have briefly discussed a wide range of security options and facilities from which application designers can choose. Although the Enterprise Java Beans may not be a large part of the system, they will be providing access to the core databases and services. Hackers and the like will exploit any small hole that exists in a system. The designers need to consider the cost of closing all known holes versus the impact of the exposure.

Chapter 5

Persistence

▼ BEAN-MANAGED PERSISTENCE
▼ CONTAINER-MANAGED PERSISTENCE

An instance of an object has, embedded within it, all the data it needs to perform its methods. In a totally object-oriented environment, the instance is responsible for its own data, and the platform is responsible for ensuring that the instance continues to be available until it is destroyed. In principle, this is exactly the same as we expect from databases; that is, they store and retain the information we write until we delete it. Persistence is the technique used in the object-oriented environment to ensure that the instance of an object continues to exist even if the computer is switched off and on again. More importantly, the instances would not be aware of this outage and would continue to be available unchanged.

The investment in existing systems means that this utopian dream of a total object-oriented environment is far from a reality. Today, we have many gigabytes of vital information about businesses held on either file systems or relational databases. In many cases, the new Enterprise Java-based systems will not be able to totally replace the existing systems and so will need to coexist or integrate with them.

Before we look at the Enterprise JavaBeans persistence model, let us look at the approaches defined in the JavaBeans architecture, which provides two important approaches for persistence and integration with existing databases. The first approach is the database access services (that is, JDBC and JSQL). These services provide an easy-to-use means of accessing a wide range of databases and filestores and are discussed further in "Java Database Connectivity (JDBC)" on page 105. The second form of persistence is the Java serialization service. If all your Beans are disposable, that is, they can be recreated simply from the data held in databases and filestores, you probably do not need to concern yourself with Java serialization. However, in many cases, you will need to use it, and it is the process used to package Enterprise Java Beans. Figure 5–1 shows two stages of the serialization model.

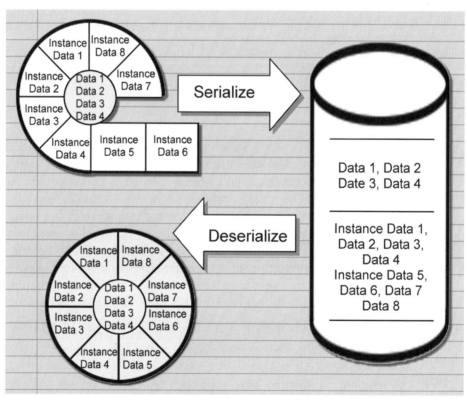

Figure 5–1 *Serialization Model*

The first stage extracts the essence of the Bean, that is, the core data and all the supporting instance and state data. This data is stored in a database or filestores. At a later stage, when the Bean needs to be recreated, this stored data is restored into another instance. The Java serialization model also accommodates the fact that objects are connected to other objects and that all the objects need to be serialized and recreated together to be usable.

Persistence is a vital piece of the Enterprise JavaBeans specification. Beans will typically implement an object view of data that is held in a database or filestore. In the Enterprise JavaBeans architecture, these objects are referred to as entity objects. Entity objects are transactional and so are recoverable if the system crashes or is restarted. They are the means by which persistence will most commonly be implemented. They either handle the persistence themselves (referred to as Bean-managed persistence) or can delegate persistence to the container (referred to as container-managed persistence).

For the entity objects to be portable across different Enterprise JavaBeans server implementations, the Entity Bean must implement a standard set of interfaces: `ebjCreate()`, `ejbDestroy()`, `ejbLoad()`, `ejbStore()`, `ebjActiviate()`, and `ejbPassivate()`. These interfaces are called by the container and move the entity object from one state to another. The entity object has three possible states.

1.   **Does not exist**.

2.   **Pooled state**. The instances have been created but do not have a specific EJB object identity. All the instances in the pool are identical and so can be assigned to any EJB object.

3.   **Ready state**. The instance has been chosen by the container to service a particular client call for which there is no other EJB object in the ready state.

Figure 5–2 shows how the container manages moving from state to state.

Let us now look at the two models for implemented Entity Beans, how they differ, and how you would choose which one to implement.

Bean-Managed Persistence

With Bean-managed persistence, the Bean developer is responsible for writing the interface to the underlying database and filestore. The main advantage of using this approach is that the Bean can be implemented in any container, and the container does not need to generate the database calls. It is expected that this approach will probably be adopted for implementing one of the interfaces to existing systems and

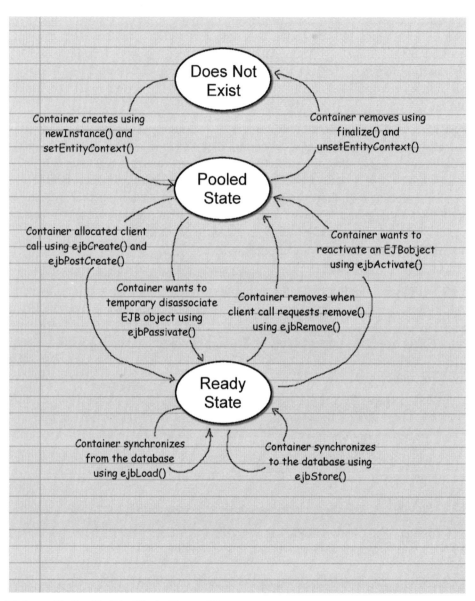

Figure 5–2 *Entity State Transition*

databases. The downside of this approach is that the interface is hard coded, so that support for different databases usually requires a rewrite of the Bean. Typically, the developer will use JDBC or JSQL to access the databases.

To implement a Bean-managed persistent entity, the developer needs to write the following methods.

- `ejbCreate()` — For getting the data from the database or filestore when the instance is first created.

- `ejbRemove()` — For writing the data back to the database or filestore when the instance is deleted.

- `ejbLoad()` — When the containers want to synchronize the data within the entity with the database or filestore.

- `ejbStore()` — When the containers update the data within the entity with the database or filestore.

- `ejbFind<method>()` — When the client makes a `find()` call, the container calls the associated `ejbFind<method>()`. At a minimum, the Bean must implement the `ejbFindPrimaryKey()` method to search the database to create a new object for a given primary key.

Container-Managed Persistence

With container-managed persistence, the Bean developer uses the container pro-vider's tools to generate the database access calls. These calls are generated at deployment time. The instance fields that will be held in the database are defined in the deployment descriptor by the `ContainerManagedFields` property.

The main advantage of this approach is that the Bean is not tightly linked to the data source. This means that the Bean should be able to support a wide variety of data sources as long as they provide all the fields required by the Bean. Also, it is anticipated that the container will provide support for a wide variety of data-stores, including:

- Relational databases using JDBC or JSQL.

- Other filestores using specific classes.

- Existing applications using classes that call the appropriate transactions or programs.

The container tools generate the same methods as were described for the Bean-managed model.

Chapter 6

Transaction Management

▼ OVERVIEW

▼ EJB SUPPORT FOR TRANSACTIONS

This chapter explains the basic concepts of transaction processing and discusses how the Enterprise JavaBeans model makes use of transaction services. By definition, "Enterprise JavaBeans defines a component model for the development and deployment of Java applications based on a multitier, distributed object architecture." The model supports distributed transactions and requires the use of a distributed transaction management system that supports the two-phase commit protocol.

Overview

Today, customers rely on object technologies to build mission-critical, distributed applications. Object technologies are the key to productivity and quality in application development. Object-oriented applications are now being deployed on commercial information processing systems where a transaction processing system provides efficient scheduling and the sharing of resources by a large number of users.

An important aspect of object technology is the "wrapping" of existing programs to allow their functions to serve as building blocks for new business applications. This technique has been successfully used to marry object-oriented, end-user interfaces with existing business applications that were developed with classical procedural techniques. A wrapper technique can similarly be used to encapsulate a large body of existing business applications on legacy systems and to leverage their functions in building new business applications. This capability will enable customers to gradually deploy object technology into their existing environments without having to redevelop all existing business functions at once.

Transactions

Transaction processing is a computing paradigm whereby many users access large quantities of information in real time without interfering with each other and without sacrificing the integrity, speed, and reliability of service provided to each user. The work of many users can be processed at the same time by a single transaction processing system or by multiple systems in a distributed computing environment. The concept of transactions was first deployed in commercial applications with centralized computers and databases. Now, it has been extended to the broader context of distributed computing and is widely accepted as the model for development of reliable distributed applications.

A transaction is defined as a set of operations that transforms data from one consistent state to another. This set of operations is an indivisible unit of work, that is, typically initiated from a user at a workstation or from some client program. The operations that make up a transaction generally consist of requests for access to existing data, requests to modify existing data, requests to add new data, or any combination of these requests. Transactions have several important characteristics, referred to as ACID properties.

- **Atomicity.** A transaction is either successful or unsuccessful. Either all of the operations that make up a transaction take effect or none take effect. A successful transaction will commit, and an unsuccessful transaction will abort. Any operations performed by an aborted transaction are undone (rolled back) so that the transaction has no effect.

- **Consistency.** A transaction transforms distributed data from one consistent state to another. The application program is responsible for ensuring consistency.

- **Isolation.** Each transaction appears to execute independently of other transactions that are running concurrently. The effects of a transaction are not visible to others until the transaction completes (commits or aborts). The transactions appear to be serialized, with two or more transactions acting as though one completed before the other began, even though they execute concurrently.

- **Durability.** Also known as permanence, this property ensures that, once completed, the effects of a transaction are permanent. A subsequent failure (such as an operating system or subsystem failure, communications failure, or hardware crash) does not cause the effects to be undone.

There can be only one of two outcomes to a transaction: the transaction is committed or the transaction is rolled back. When a transaction is committed, the implication is that the transaction processing completed successfully and all changes made by the associated requests are made permanent. When a transaction is rolled back, the implication is that the transaction failed to complete normal processing and all changes made by the associated requests are undone.

Transactions are typically managed by a system component known as a transaction manager. The transaction manager implements all services to guarantee the ACID properties of a transaction. The transaction manager typically resides within an infrastructure, such as an application server or transaction processing system.

Transaction Processing

Modern transaction processing systems are increasingly complex, decentralized, and dynamic. They take advantage of evolving technologies to stay competitive and to benefit from smaller, cheaper, and more powerful computers and the proliferation of communication services. At the same time, a transaction processing system has to cope with the interaction of different types of computers, communication networks, and user devices. A transaction may involve operations on a customer's notebook computer, a branch desktop computer, and a central mainframe, yet the system must still provide optimum service and integrity. In a transaction processing system, the application is completely unconcerned about where operations are performed as long as the service and integrity are maintained.

An industry-standard model for transaction processing is based on the X/Open XA protocol. X/Open is a consortium of users, software vendors, and hardware vendors who define programming interfaces. This model is known as the Distributed Transaction Processing (DTP) model and is illustrated in Figure 6–1.

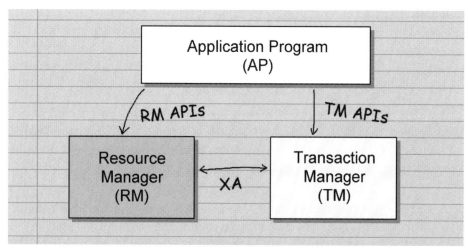

Figure 6–1 *Distributed Transaction Processing (DTP) Model*

Distributed Transaction Processing

Distributed transaction processing ensures that application processing can span multiple databases on multiple systems coordinated by multiple transaction managers.

Transaction processing in a distributed system environment requires the cooperation of three different components: the transaction manager (TM), which serves as the transaction coordinator by providing transaction services to the applications; the resource manager (RM), which participates in the transaction by performing work on behalf of the applications; and the application program, whose business logic requires transaction services. Each of these roles contributes to the Distributed Transaction Processing (DTP) system by implementing different sets of transaction API and functionality.

Transaction Manager

The transaction manager is typically a system component of an application server or transaction processing system. The application server provides the infrastructure required to support the application execution environment. The transaction manager implements a set of low-level transaction interfaces that are not exposed to the applications. The low-level transaction services allow the TM to coordinate transaction processing performed by multiple resource managers, such as database connections, messaging sessions, or connections to backend legacy systems on behalf of the application. Transaction context is propagated by the TM to all resource managers that participate in the transaction, even across network connections. An example of low-level transaction services is the API provided by Java

Transaction Service (JTS). JTS is a mapping of the OMG Object Transaction Service (OTS) specification to the Java programming language.

The JTS API is a low-level transaction management service intended for vendors who provide a transaction system infrastructure for application runtime execution. An EJB server vendor can use JTS to provide transaction services on behalf of transactional applications, such as EJB applications.

The transaction manager (TM) manages global transactions and coordinates the decision to commit them or roll them back, thus ensuring atomic transaction completion. The TM also coordinates recovery activities of the resource managers when necessary, such as after a component fails.

Resource Manager

The resource manager (RM) supports distributed transactions by implementing a transaction resource interface, and it participates in transactions that are externally controlled by a TM. An example of a resource manager interface is the industry-standard X/Open XA protocol. The X/Open XA protocol is supported by most database vendors and is also used by messaging or communications systems, such as MQSeries.

In the X/Open DTP model, RMs structure any changes to the resources they manage as part of a recoverable, atomic transaction. The RM lets the TM coordinate completion of the atomic transaction with work done by other RMs.

Application Program

The application program (AP) performs the business logic of a transaction. A component-based transactional application that is developed to operate in a modern application server environment typically does not need to contain any transaction logic. An example of a modern application server environment is the industry-standard Enterprise JavaBeans (EBJ) component architecture, which is defined by the EJB 1.0 Specifications.

In some cases, it may be desirable for a client program or an Enterprise Java Bean to manage transaction scope. The Enterprise JavaBeans architecture implements this capability through an interface that is defined as part of the Java Transaction API (JTA).

The AP implements the desired function of the end-user enterprise. Each AP specifies a sequence of operations that may involve resources, such as a database, file, or interoperation with a legacy system. An AP defines the start and end of a global transaction, accesses resources within transaction boundaries, and usually decides whether to commit or roll back each transaction.

EJB Support for Transactions

Enterprise JavaBeans are typically transactional and execute within a distributed transaction processing environment. EJB developers can write applications that use multiple resource managers that are possibly distributed across systems in a network environment. Since the burden of managing transactions is provided through containers and EJB servers, EJB developers are not exposed to the complexity of distributed transactions. The EJB containers and servers implement the necessary APIs, low-level transaction services, and protocols to support the transaction processing requirements of the EJB.

Enterprise JavaBeans supports transactions modeled after the OMG Object Transaction Service (OTS) for flat transactions. The OMG OTS model for flat transactions is based on the X/Open DTP definition of transaction function and commitment protocols. A flat transaction is a top-level transaction that cannot create a child transaction. By contrast, the OTS specification defines support for a nested transaction model.

Nested transactions allow an application to create a transaction that is encompassed in an existing transaction providing for a finer granularity of recovery. The effect of failures that require rollback can be limited so that unaffected parts of the transaction are not rolled back. The EJB 1.0 specification does not support nested transactions.

EJB Transaction Management

Enterprise JavaBeans is a high-level component framework that masks system complexity from the application developer. Therefore, most Enterprise Java Beans and their clients do not need direct access to transaction management APIs. Transaction management services are provided by the EJB container and server on behalf of the EJB. This form of transaction management is commonly referred to as implicit transaction management.

In the event that clients and Enterprise Java Beans need direct access to transaction management services (for example, explicit transaction management), an interface is available through the Java Transaction API (JTA). This interface is called the `javax.transaction.UserTransaction` interface. It is intended to be used by both the EJB provider (for `TX_BEAN_MANAGED` Beans) and the client programmer who wants to explicitly demarcate transaction boundaries within Java programs. The `javax.transaction.UserTransaction` interface is the only interface that an EJB container or EJB server vendor is required to implement in order to support EJBs.

The EJB 1.0 specification does not reflect a change in packaging for Java transaction management APIs. The `javax.jts.UserTransaction` interface and the

`XAResource` interface have been removed from the JTS API and are now packaged as part of JTA. As part of repackaging, `javax.jts.UserTransaction` interface has been renamed the `javax.transaction.UserTransaction` interface.

The JTA and JTS APIs define all the Java programming language interfaces related to transaction management on a Java platform.

Java Transaction API

The Java Transaction API consists of two elements: a high-level application transaction demarcation interface and a standard Java mapping of the X/Open XA protocol.

- **User Transaction Interface.** The application transaction demarcation interface, `javax.transaction.UserTransaction`, allows an application programmer to control transaction boundaries explicitly. This interface is implemented by an EJB container to support Bean-managed EJB components and to allow Java client programs to demarcate transaction boundaries through programming.

- **XA Resource Interface.** The `XAResource` interface is a standard X/Open XA interface. The API enables attachment of a resource manager (such as a JDBC or JMS driver) to an external transaction manager. A potential use for this API is to allow an EJB container or server provider to interface with a JDBC driver.

Java Transaction Service

The Java Transaction Service (JTS) API consists of low-level, transaction management APIs intended for vendors who provide a transaction system infrastructure to support an application runtime environment. It consists of a standard Java mapping of the OMG Object Transaction Service (OTS) 1.1 interfaces. The API is intended for a CORBA application or system programmer using the Java language. The API provides the programmer with several interfaces, including transaction demarcation and transaction propagation.

Support for this API is not required in the EJB environment. A vendor can choose to use this API as part of the interface between the EJB server and container but can use another API as well.

Distributed Transaction Processing

As previously mentioned, Enterprise JavaBeans is a component model designed to support distributed transactions and requires the use of a distributed transaction management system that supports the two-phase commit protocol. The model supports distributed transactions that can span multiple databases on multiple systems coordinated by multiple transaction managers. The EJB model for distributed transaction processing ensures that its transactions can interoperate with other EJB servers.

Several scenarios are illustrated in this section to demonstrate the distributed processing capabilities of Enterprise JavaBeans.

Update of Multiple Databases

Enterprise JavaBeans makes it possible for an application program to update data in multiple databases within a single transaction. To illustrate this capability, we extended the DTP model (Figure 6–2) to represent an EJB server environment.

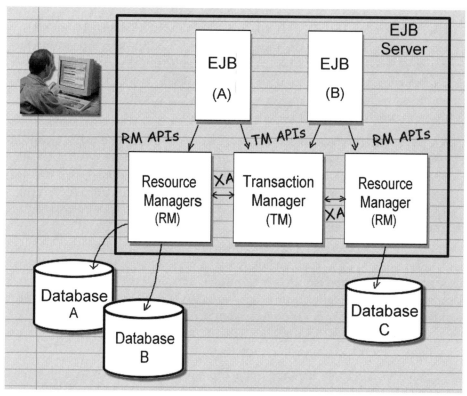

Figure 6–2 *Update of Multiple Databases*

The above scenario depicts multiple databases being updated within the same transaction by two Enterprise Java Beans. A request from a client results in two Enterprise Java Beans being invoked within the same transaction. EJB (A) updates two databases, then invokes EJB (B), which updates a single database. The Enterprise Java Beans perform the database updates through the JDBC API, and the

EJB server manages the database connections. When the transaction completes, the EJB server and the underlying DBMS(s) perform a two-phase commit to ensure atomic update across all databases involved in the transaction. The EJB developer does not have to be concerned about the transactional (ACID) properties of the transaction.

Update Across Multiple EJB Servers

Enterprise JavaBeans makes it possible for Enterprise Java Beans to update databases across multiple EJB servers within the same transaction. The EJB servers can be network connected and located at different sites. This capability is illustrated in Figure 6–3.

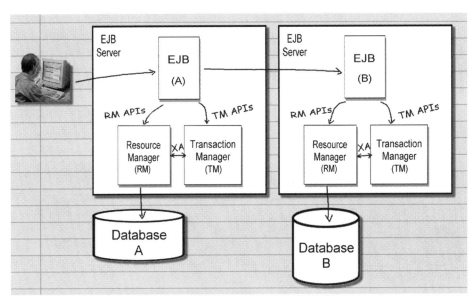

Figure 6–3 *Update Across Multiple Systems*

The above scenario depicts two databases being updated within the same transaction across two EJB servers on different systems. A request from a client results in two Enterprise Java Beans being invoked within the same transaction. EJB (A) updates a database, then invokes EJB (B), which updates another database on another EJB server. The EJB servers are located on different systems that are connected through a network. The two EJB servers propagate the transaction context from EJB (A) to EJB (B). When the transaction completes, the two servers use a distributed two-phase commit protocol to ensure the atomic property of the transaction. The propagation of transaction context, as well as other ACID properties of the transaction, are transparent to the EJB developer.

Interoperability with Non-Java Clients and Servers

In some cases, it may be desirable for Enterprise Java Beans to interoperate with non-Java clients and servers. An example of a non-Java client is a CORBA client, and an example of a non-Java server might be a legacy system.

An EJB server can make it possible for an Enterprise Java Bean to be invoked from a non-Java client, such as a CORBA client. The EJB-to-CORBA mapping allows any CORBA client to invoke an Enterprise Java Bean on a CORBA-enabled server.

Another important aspect of distributed transaction processing for Enterprise JavaBeans is the capability to connect to existing applications or legacy systems. This capability may be implemented by the EJB server through a bridge or connector. For instance, a bridge can make it possible for an Enterprise Java Bean to interoperate with an existing program on another system. The bridge can make the program visible to the Enterprise Java Bean as if there was a Bean in some container on another EJB server. On a Java platform, a vendor may choose to use JDBC, JMS, or some other transactional protocol (such as OSI TP or SNA LU6.2) to implement the bridge.

The illustration in Figure 6–4 shows EJB interoperability with non-Java clients and servers.

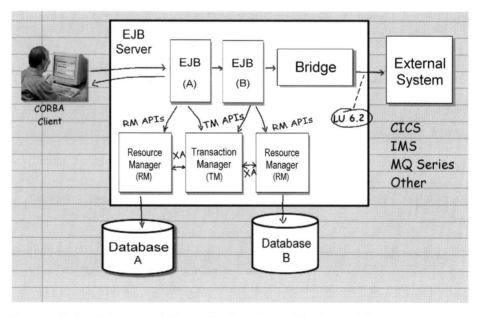

Figure 6–4 *Interoperability with Non-Java Clients and Servers*

In the above scenario, a CORBA client invokes an Enterprise Java Bean on an EJB server. The CORBA client is written in a CORBA-supported language, such as Visual Basic or C++. The EJB server supports the client request just like a request from a pure Java client, through the EJB-to-CORBA mapping. (See "Three-Tier Distributed Computing Model" for more details.)

Another aspect of this scenario is EJB access to an existing system. In this case, the second Enterprise Java Bean (EJB (B)) makes a request to an existing system through a bridge supplied by the EJB server vendor. In this case, the bridge is a mapping of the LU6.2 protocol that provides access CICS, IMS, MQSeries, or some other LU6.2-based application. A mapping of the LU6.2 protocol should include support for two-phase commit, rollback, and transaction identifiers.

All processing for the client request is managed within the same transaction context, including access to the legacy system.

Declarative Transaction Management

When a client method is invoked on an Enterprise JavaBean object, the method is interposed by the container. This interposition enables the Enterprise JavaBean object to delegate transaction management to the container. The declarative transaction management is controlled by a transaction attribute that is associated with each Enterprise JavaBean home container.

The attribute for each Enterprise Java Bean is defined by a descriptor and is associated with the Bean's home container during deployment. The container provider should provide tools to set the transaction attribute value during deployment and to change the value after deployment.

The transaction attribute value for an Enterprise Java Bean can be specified for the entire Bean or for individual methods of the Bean. Six values are defined by Enterprise JavaBeans for the transaction attribute.

- `TX_NOT_SUPPORTED`. The Enterprise JavaBean object is invoked without a transaction scope by the container when this attribute value is specified.

- `TX_BEAN_MANAGED`. The Enterprise JavaBean object can use the `javax.transaction.UserTransaction` interface to demarcate transaction boundaries.

- `TX_REQUIRED`. The Enterprise JavaBean object is invoked by the container with a transaction context. If a client has a transaction context when it invokes the Enterprise JavaBean object; the method call uses the client's transaction context. If the client does not have a transaction context, the container starts a new transaction for the method call.

- TX_SUPPORTS. The Enterprise JavaBean object can be invoked within the transaction context of the client. If the client does not have a transaction context, the Bean object is invoked without a transaction context.

- TX_REQUIRES_NEW. The Enterprise JavaBean object is invoked with a new transaction context. The container always starts a new transaction for the method call. If the client has a transaction context when the Enterprise Java Bean's method is called, the client's transaction is suspended before the new transaction is started and resumed when the new transaction has completed.

- TX_MANDATORY. The Enterprise JavaBean object is always invoked within the client's transaction context. If the client does not have a transaction context, the container throws the TransactionRequired exception and the method call fails.

Transaction Demarcation

The Enterprise JavaBeans model provides three techniques for management of transaction scope or demarcation of transactions: client-managed demarcation, container-managed demarcation, and Bean-managed demarcation. A brief explanation of each technique is provided below.

Client-Managed Demarcation

The javax.transaction.UserTransaction interface allows a client or a nontransactional EJB object to explicitly demarcate transaction boundaries. This capability is illustrated in Figure 6–5.

In this scenario, the client program uses explicit demarcation to perform atomic updates across multiple databases that reside on different EJB servers. The client program issues the begin call, then invokes EJB (A), which updates database A. The client program then invokes EJB (B), which updates database B. The commit call is issued by the client program when database processing has been completed for both EJBs. The EJB servers ensure that updates to the databases are transactional. A proxy of a transaction service on the client automatically propagates the transaction context to the two EJB servers. When the client program issues the commit, the two EJB servers perform the two-phase commit operation. The capability for client-managed demarcation is provided through the EJB-to-CORBA mapping of transactions.

Container-Managed Demarcation

When a client program invokes an Enterprise Java Bean, the container interposes on the method invocation, which enables the container to control transaction demarcation through its transaction attribute.

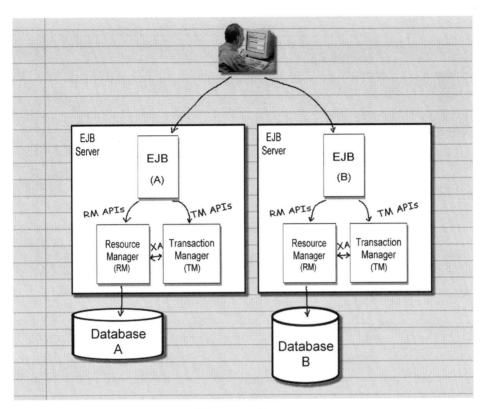

Figure 6–5   *Client-Managed Demarcation*

For instance, assume that an Enterprise JavaBean object is deployed with the
TX_REQUIRED attribute and is invoked by a nontransactional client (for exam-
ple, the client does not have a transaction context). This scenario is illustrated in
Figure 6–6.

This scenario depicts an Enterprise JavaBean object being invoked by a nontransactional client. Since the client does not have a transaction context, the container
creates a new transaction before dispatching the remote method on EJB (A). EJB
(A) updates a database, then invokes EJB (B), which also updates a database. The
processing performed by both Enterprise Java Beans is done within the same
transaction context, subject to the transaction attribute of EJB (B).

The scenario assumes that EJB (B) has an appropriate transaction attribute value.
In this case, the transaction attribute value of EJB (B) cannot be
TX_NOT_SUPPORTED or TX_REQUIRES_NEW.

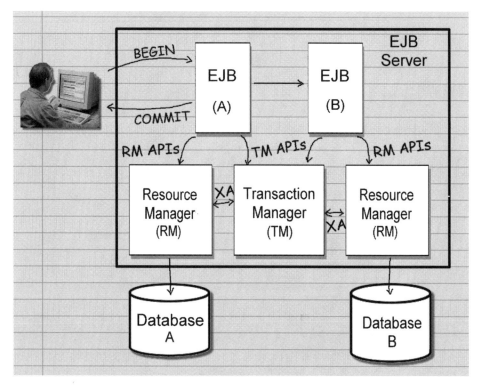

Figure 6–6 *Container-Managed Demarcation*

Bean-Managed Demarcation

Bean-managed demarcation is allowed when an Enterprise Java Bean is deployed with a transaction attribute of TX_BEAN_MANAGED. In this case, the Bean can use the javax.transaction.UserTransaction interface for transaction demarcation. The container makes the interface available to the Enterprise Java Bean through the EJBContext.getUserTransaction() method, which is illustrated in the following snippet of code.

```
import javax.transaction.UserTransaction;
...
EJBContext ic = ...;
...
UserTransaction tx = ic.getUserTransaction();
tx.begin();
... // business logic
tx.commit();
```

Enterprise Java Beans deployed with an attribute other than `TX_BEAN_MANAGED` are not allowed to use this interface. The container ensures that the `javax.transaction.UserTransaction` interface is unavailable to these Enterprise Java Beans.

Note that there are special considerations for stateful Session Beans when the `TX_BEAN_MANAGED` transaction attribute is specified. For instance, it is legal for a stateful Session Bean to retain an association with a transaction across multiple calls from a client. This retention occurs when a business method that initiated the transaction returns without completing (for example, committing or rolling back) the transaction. In this case, the container must retain the association between the transaction and the instance of the stateful Session Bean. The association is retained across multiple client calls until the transaction completes.

Unlike a stateful Session Bean, an instance of a stateless Session Bean or an Entity Bean is not allowed to retain an association across method calls. This means that if a business method initiates a transaction, the method must complete (commit or roll back) the transaction before it returns.

Transaction Isolation

Each Enterprise Java Bean must have a specification for its transaction isolation level. This information is specified as part of the deployment descriptor and is used by the container as follows.

- For Session Beans and Entity Beans with Bean-managed persistence, the container ensures that the specified transaction isolation level is set on the database connections used by the Bean at the start of each transaction.

- For Entity Beans with container-managed persistence, the database access calls generated by the container tools must achieve the specified isolation level.

Transaction Isolation Levels

Four transaction isolation-level values can be specified by the Enterprise Java Bean provided as part of the deployment descriptor. The possible values that can be specified are:

- `TX_READ_UNCOMMITTED`

- `TX_READ_COMMITTED`

- `TRANSACTION_REPEATABLE_READ`

- `TRANSACTION_SERIALIZABLE`

Transaction isolation-level values can be specified for the entire Enterprise Java-Beans or for its individual Bean methods. If a value is specified on an individual method, the value takes precedence over the value specified at the Bean level.

Chapter 7

Development
and Deployment

▼ ROLES IN THE DEVELOPMENT AND
  DEPLOYMENT PHASE

▼ STAGES IN DEVELOPING AND DEPLOYING

Enterprise JavaBeans promises to make real the dream of component-based development. It is expected that component providers will develop collections of components or frameworks. Customers will customize these frameworks and integrate them into their current environment. This chapter looks at the roles in developing and deploying Enterprise Java Beans.

Roles in the Development and Deployment Phase

There are six roles in the development of Enterprise JavaBeans:

- Enterprise JavaBean provider

- Deployer

- Application assembler

- Enterprise JavaBeans server provider

- Enterprise JavaBeans container provider

- System administrator

These roles are described in detail in the Enterprise JavaBeans Specification V1.0 document.

Although a number of roles are defined, one or more roles may be performed by a single person or group.

Enterprise JavaBean Provider

The Enterprise JavaBean provider is responsible for writing new classes that conform to the Enterprise JavaBeans specification. These Beans will implement a set of business functions or entities to solve a particular business need.

This provider typically has extensive business knowledge and is not an expert in low-level systems programming. As such, the provider will depend on the EJB container provider to provide the transactional infrastructure, that is, the transaction management, concurrency, security, and distribution. However, the provider must define transactional requirements of the classes. Therefore, the provider must understand the EJB architecture and the facilities that are available.

The provider defines the client interface for the Beans. This interface defines the methods that clients can use to invoke the business functions.

The provider will shrink-wrap the Beans by creating an EJB Jar file (see "The EJB Jar File" on page 97).

Deployer

The deployer installs on a server the classes developed by the provider. To assist in the installation, the deployer uses any tools provided by the container provider to customize the Enterprise Java Beans to specific requirements. The tools typically create containers specifically for these Beans. Also, the remote implementation of the EJBHome EJBObject interfaces must be created by providers' tools.

The deployer must understand the specific operational requirements of the class, for example, the entity-to-database mapping, security definitions. "Deploying Enterprise Java Beans" on page 98 provides a more detailed description of the deployment process.

Application Assembler

The application assemblers create overall business applications using the Enterprise Java Beans. They typically integrate a number of Beans into a single client application by using the Bean's client contract. The assembler only needs to be familiar with the interface provided by the Beans and the associated business functionality. The assembler does not need to be familiar with the details of building Enterprise Java Beans unless a new Enterprise Java Bean is being created.

If the interface for the Enterprise Java Beans is clearly defined prior to development, the application assembly can be done in parallel with or before the Bean development.

Server Provider

The Enterprise JavaBeans server providers should be experienced in creating distributed transaction management and distributed object systems. They provide the framework in which containers can be executed. They also provide tools to create the containers. They should provide containers that implement the session container contract and also provide entity containers for the databases and filestores that are supported.

The server provider should also provide documentation on the lower-level interfaces so that other developers can create containers for the server. Currently, there is no standard interface between containers and servers.

Container Provider

The container providers create the scalable, secure, transactional container system. They are responsible for providing the infrastructure in which the Enterprise Java Beans will execute, and they deliver the EJB specifications that the Bean developers will use (that is, the Enterprise JavaBeans component contract).

The container provider must also provide the tools that will be used to generate the code that interfaces the Enterprise Java Beans to the databases or existing applications. These interfaces apply only to container-managed Entity Beans.

The container provider should also support the version management of Enterprise Java Beans. For example, the container may allow dynamic updating or upgrading of Beans without impacting existing clients.

Using containers potentially allows an organization to choose the server and the containers separately. This separation could prove invaluable in integrating multiple EJB frameworks and also migrating from one server to another.

System Administrator

The system administrator is responsible for keeping the system up and running. The administrator uses the tools provided by the server and container providers to assist in this job. It is also anticipated that the system management tool vendors, such as Tivoli or Hewlett-Packard's OpenView, will provide tools to assist in managing EJBs.

Stages in Developing and Deploying

There are three separate stages to the development of Enterprise JavaBeans.

1. **Design and develop the classes themselves.** These are packaged into a framework for marketing and deployment. This framework is physically packaged in a standard Java programming language Archive file, referred to as an EJB Jar file.

2. **Customize and deploy the Enterprise Java Beans.** Typically, the deployer uses the EJB Jar files and the container tools to create the containers of the implementation to the specific server.

3. **Design and develop the applications.** Typically, the frameworks come with a JavaDoc that is used by the application assemblers to build the overall application.

This section discusses the first two stages in more detail, as they are unique to Enterprise JavaBeans development.

Figure 7–1 shows the stages of developing Enterprise JavaBeans.

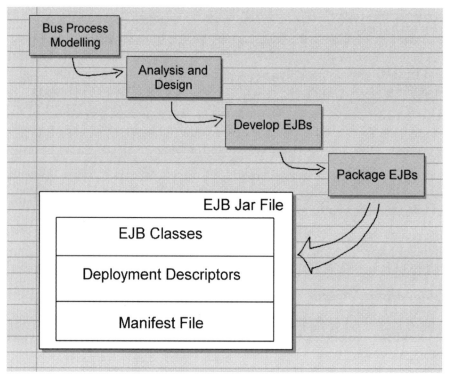

Figure 7–1   *Stages in Developing Enterprise JavaBeans*

The initial design and development of the Enterprise JavaBeans classes would be the same for any other object-oriented business application development. Once an Enterprise JavaBeans provider has completed development of the Beans, he packages them into a file. This package is provided to deployers as an EJB Jar file. The Jar file is the standard means by which EJB vendors provide reusable components.

The EJB Jar File

The EJB Jar file includes the following.

- **The Enterprise JavaBeans class files** —These classes are used by the deployer to create the containers and implement the Beans.

- **The deployment descriptors** —These are the means by which the Bean developer provides the Bean deployer with an implementation checklist. This descriptor is a standard form that it is portable between different environments.

  The deployment descriptor contains serialized copies of the session and entity descriptor objects. These descriptors include the following information for each class:

  - Transaction attributes — A Bean-level definition of transactional behavior. These are six defined behaviors, ranging from not supported to mandatory and including a Bean-managed option.

  - Security — The access control and identification attributes. For example, an attribute defines whether the Bean should assume the identity of the calling client, the server, or a different entity.

  - EJB environment properties — Properties that the developer wants the deployer to customize, for example, the location of a database on specific global constants.

  - Class names of the EJB classes — The names that are stored in the JNDI database.

  - Home and remote interfaces details — Names of the classes that implement the Bean's home and remote interfaces.

  - Name of the primary key type — Defines a unique key that identifies that instance. For example, an Entity Bean would have a primary key that would identify the row of a table that it represents.

  - Container-managed fields — List of all the Beans that are managed by the container.

Refer to the Enterprise JavaBeans specification for a more detailed discussion of the contents of the descriptor.

- **The EJB Jar manifest file** —The file declares all the Beans in the EJB Jar file. Every Bean must have an entry in the manifest file in the form of:

```
Name: <the relative name of the Bean's serialized deployment descriptor>
Enterprise-Bean: <value of TRUE>
```

This entry declares a Bean as an Enterprise Java Bean.

Deploying Enterprise Java Beans

Deployment involves receiving an EJB Jar file and creating on an Enterprise Java server the container in which the Jar file will execute. The Enterprise Java Beans must also be customized for the specific implementation. The container provider should provide tools to perform the following tasks.

- **Read the EJB Jar file.** The tool should deserialize the deployment descriptors and use this deserialization to create a default implementation of the Beans. It should then generate the container-specific classes and the stub and skeletons for distributed objects. The Bean's home interface will be defined in JNDI to enable client access.

- **Manage the deployment descriptor attribute.** The deployer must modify the deployment descriptor attributes loaded from the EJB Jar file. The container provider should provide tools to manage these deployments. These tools must also enforce any specific restrictions based on the server and the container.

- **Customize the business logic.** Optionally, the container provider will provide tools to allow the deployer to customize the business logic. The EJB specification has not defined this customization, to allow suppliers maximum freedom.

- **Map the container-managed persistence fields to the data source.** A container supports a specific set of databases or legacy application sources. Therefore, the container vendor must provide appropriate tools to map the container-managed fields to the appropriate data sources.

Chapter **8**

The Future of Enterprise JavaBeans

▼ WISH LIST FOR ENTERPRISE JAVABEANS

▼ EXPERTS' PREDICTIONS ABOUT
ENTERPRISE JAVABEANS

The focus of Enterprise JavaBeans Release 1.0 architecture is to define the basic component model for Session and Entity Enterprise Java Beans. The model includes the distributed object model, Enterprise JavaBeans application programming model, and state and transaction management protocols.

Wish List for Enterprise JavaBeans

Given the broad scope of the Enterprise JavaBeans specification, we defer to future releases the features that introduce an advanced programmer's style. This conservative approach reduces the chance of our having to make a backward, incompatible change in a future release.

Examples of the features that we want to consider for a later release are listed below.

- **Programmatic access to security.** We would like to allow expert-level Enterprise Java Beans to manage their security identity.

- **A serialized Bean prototype.** In EJB 1.0, an Enterprise Java Bean can only be a Java class, not a serialized Java object. We want to investigate if there is value in allowing a serialized object to qualify as an Enterprise Java Bean.

- **Client capability to obtain a URL string from an Enterprise JavaBean object reference.**

- **A standard API between the EJB server and EJB container.**

Experts' Predictions About Enterprise JavaBeans

Where Will EJB Go?

(Reference: *Network Computing World Article*
http://www.ncworldmag.com/ncworld/ncw-01-1998/ncw-01-ejbeans.html)

We can predict that software companies will release libraries (or hills) of Beans for use by application developers just like those application-specific widget classes found in some visual IDEs for the C++ language. With this application, developers will have to get their hands on these Beans to start creating real network applications.

Competitively, Microsoft's Distributed InterNet Architecture (DNA) is an evolution of its DCOM/ActiveX model that aims to provide a similar, although proprietary, mechanism. Microsoft is also a step ahead with plans to develop industry-specific vertical versions of DNA, such as DNA for financial services, health management, manufacturing, and so on. Each DNA provides not only the basic architecture but also supporting code specific to the needs of these industry sectors.

All in all, EJB is a step in the right direction for Java and for network-centric computing. It will provide the framework for future Java-based applications that can rival the major applications of today while still providing a large number of advantages over current systems and models. In an upcoming article, we'll discuss the internals of Enterprise Java Beans and discover how they work.

On the Horizon

Reference: *The WebSphere Application Server Architecture and Programming model, IBM Systems Journal Article*

As Java picks up momentum and a greater mindshare, it will become more and more accepted as "enterprise ready." Looming on the horizon are Enterprise Java Beans. EJBs are transaction-ready, scalable Java Beans paving the way for doing heavy-duty enterprise applications in the NCF. JDK 1.2 promises to add performance as well as a slew of additional APIs. The Java Servlet Development Kit

(JSDK) will be a standard extension of Version 1.2 as well as JIDL, the Java interface definition language, for supporting CORBA objects, JMAPI, the Java Management API, and JNDI, the Java Naming and Directory Interface.

The reasons for choosing Java as the basis of the NCF programming model are very concrete. There is definitely benefit from the fact that Java has a lot of mindshare in the Internet space, but in addition to that, many technical reasons make Java a compelling choice for NCF applications.

- **Portability.** Although the Java promise of "write once, run everywhere" is not yet completely fulfilled, Java is by far the most portable language yet. There are still differences in the Java virtual machines on different platforms and by different vendors, but these differences are slowly going away. Sun's "100% Pure Java" initiative and set of comprehensive test suites are making the bridge between platforms and vendors smaller and smaller. Although some have suggested that the Java promise is "Write once, test everywhere," that approach is still much more productive than the porting nightmares associated with C and C++ applications.

- **Functionality.** Java is not only a language, but more and more a programming environment. Java is building in powerful functions, such as JDBC, JavaBeans, and JTS, making it a functional and powerful development platform.

- **Performance.** Because servlets are persistent, reducing startup and destroying overhead, and because they run in the same process as the Web server, they typically run several times faster than CGI programs.

- **Security and Reliability.** The Java virtual machine restricts servlets from accessing server resources, and through the use of a security manager, an administrator can impose restrictions on running servlets, making the Web server more secure and reliable. Current Web server APIs, such as Internet Server API (ISAPI) and Netscape Server API (NSAPI), could crash and corrupt the hosting Web server. The built-in security mechanism of Java is now considerably revamped with the introduction of the JDK 1.2 security model.

- **Consistency.** One of the primary goals of the NCF was to follow consistent industry standards. The "Web revolution" was spurred by interoperability based on a simple standard (HTML and HTTP). Java has shown great promise as a consistent standard; the 100% Pure Java program ensures interoperability on all platforms, and comprehensive test suites exist to ensure that vendor implementations of the virtual machine adhere to the JavaSoft specification.

Industry Directions

Reference: *The Promise of EJB, DBMS Online Article*
http://www.dbmsmag.com/9808d18.html

EJB breathes new life into CORBA. The CORBA infrastructure is readily adaptable to supporting EJB, and Sun acknowledged the importance of leveraging that infrastructure by publishing an EJB-to-CORBA mapping specification in conjunction with the EJB specification. Under this model, vendors are using plumbing built for CORBA but emphasizing the EJB component model over CORBA's object model. EJB servers built on CORBA generate CORBA IDL implicitly in the runtime environment; the developer never sees any CORBA coding. The mapping specification addresses mapping EJB interfaces to IDL over the Internet Inter-Orb Protocol (IIOP), mapping EJB object names to the CORBA name service, mapping EJB transactions to the OTS, and resolving client identity for security purposes.

Inprise, Oracle, and Novera are building their EJB support on existing or new CORBA services. Inprise is adding EJB runtime support to its VisiBroker product line, which has been established in the CORBA world for some time. Version 4.0 of Oracle's application server is primarily a CORBA server that manages EJB through the CORBA-to-EJB mapping protocols. Likewise, Novera is building its jBusiness suite on a CORBA foundation.

These vendors and others are differentiating themselves in a variety of ways. Oracle will build EJB container support into both its application server and version 8.3 of the RDBMS itself; in addition, Oracle will support executing EJB-based logic on the client. Oracle is offering extreme flexibility in deploying EJBs to satisfy the requirements of a diverse customer population that scales from small to large enterprises. On the applications side, Oracle is redesigning its ERP suite so it is based on Designer/2000 models that emit logic as EJBs through Developer/2000. Oracle believes that this approach will yield a stronger implementation and customization story than SAP's; EJB is a more robust and standard architecture than SAP's BAPI, and model-based EJB generation will pervade the entire product rather than selected exposed components. Using EJB lets application developers, such as Oracle, focus on packaged business logic and rely on a standard infrastructure for handling security, transactions, and partitioning.

Novera's jBusiness family of products includes Component Development Environment, an Application Server, and a Management Server. The development environment will drop into existing IDEs and includes a wizard that generates EJBs from classes that a developer builds, based on his answers to a series of questions about the EJB's desired behavior. The EJB container will run in the application server, which will support OTS transactions, load balancing, and failover among multiple server instances. Multiweight client access will let powerful clients download and execute business objects locally and interoperate with the server through RPCs. EJB support in the management server includes the ability to view types active in the container, statistics, and an agent scheme based on the event service. It provides these services by introducing management daemon objects into the application server runtime environment.

Persistence Software Inc. claims that its EJB-enabled application server, PowerTier for EJB, will be the fastest application server available. It leverages the company's patented object caching technology to accelerate the Java application performance as well as Persistence's object-to-relational mapping technology, which lets the server load frequently used data into in-memory objects at startup. Persistence has implemented an interesting model for managing changing data (for example, changes in the state of persistent objects). The PowerTier server isolates uncommitted client changes by creating a private transactional cache that holds the changed objects for each client application. Other users continue to work with the unchanged object in the shared cache. Once a client's work has been committed and accepted by the database, the changed objects are copied from the private transactional cache back into the shared cache.

WebLogic's Tengah application server supports all the optional features described in the EJB specifications. These include distributed transactions, the ability to start transactions on the client or the server and propagate them to other servers, and automatic persistence of both Session and Entity Beans based on the JDBC specification. WebLogic positions the Tengah server as a fully JPE-based server rather than a CORBA-based EJB container and focuses heavily on providing optimized versions of the supporting JPE APIs, including JDBC and RMI. The resulting architecture makes it easy for EJB developers to take advantage of services, such as Tengah Events and load balancing.

In WebLogic's view, RMI is the appropriate protocol for coordinating distributed objects because it's very useful to have a protocol that passes objects as arguments to other objects on the network. WebLogic replaces the JavaSoft reference implementation of RMI with its own Tengah RMI. Tengah RMI makes coding distributed solutions easier than using JavaSoft's reference implementation. For example, a remote method does not need to declare RemoteException, and Tengah RMI does not require a separate stub and skeleton class for every remote class. Additionally, there is no requirement in Tengah RMI to set a security manager because all of Tengah RMI's services are provided in the context of the secure Tengah server. Likewise, WebLogic's Tengah RMI offers flexibility among several schemes for naming, binding, and looking up remote objects. URLs can use the standard `rmi://` scheme, or they can take advantage of other protocols like

HTTP, which lets Tengah RMI function across firewalls that restrict all messages but HTTP.

Java applications and EJBs hosted by Tengah can be replicated with no additional programming. For scalability, Tengah automatically balances the load across available instances of the replicated service and provides a console for remotely monitoring and updating the state of your Tengah application and server cluster. To ensure fault tolerance, Tengah also replicates state information so that an outage can be completely masked from both the user and application. Tengah includes a publish-and-subscribe model for synchronizing applications and data sets over a network.

Future Relationship to JTS

Reference: *JavaSoft EJB Specifications, page 96*

A Java programming language mapping of the standard X/Open XA interface. This is an API for attaching a resource manager (such as JDBC driver) to an external transaction manager. An EJB server or container could use this API to interface to the database drivers. This API is being proposed and reviewed as part of the JDBC 2.0 specification.

Chapter 9

Technology

▼ JAVA DATABASE CONNECTIVITY (JDBC)

▼ JAVA TRANSACTIONS

▼ JAVA NAMING AND DIRECTORY INTERFACE (JNDI)

▼ REMOTE METHOD INVOCATION (RMI)

▼ SERVLETS

▼ JAVASERVER PAGES

This chapter describes a number of technologies that complement EJB and might be used in an EJB-based enterprise solution.

Java Database Connectivity (JDBC)

Persistency, the ability to store the current state of a program and then to restore the program to its previously stored state if restarted at a later time, is one of the key requirements of EJB Entity Beans. For an Entity Bean with Bean-managed persistence, an Enterprise JavaBean provider might use the Java Database Connectivity (JDBC) API to provide the persistence.

The JDBC API is a standard Java interface for access to relational databases. It allows a programmer to write vendor-independent code that can issue queries and process the results for a wide choice of database engines. JDBC is similar in concept to Microsoft's Open Database Connectivity (ODBC). Both implementations are based on the same specification, the X/Open SQL Call Level interface.

A Java program using JDBC can communicate with databases from different vendors by using an appropriate JDBC driver. Multiple database connections are allowed, as illustrated in Figure 9–1, but all the necessary JDBC drivers must be loaded first.

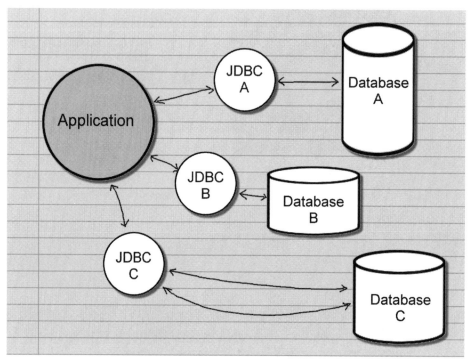

Figure 9–1   *Example of JDBC Connections*

Java programs that access databases by using the JDBC API go through a common flow of events to get access to database resources, as described in detail in the sections that follow.

1. Load the target database JDBC driver.

2. Connect to the database.

3. Execute SQL statements.

Loading a JDBC Driver

JDBC achieves platform independence by providing a driver manager that dynamically maintains all the driver objects. The driver objects are registered with the driver manager at their loading time, and the programmer forces the loading by using the `Class.forName()` method. For example, to connect to an ODBC database, the JDBC-ODBC bridge driver must first be loaded. This loading can be achieved by the following piece of code.

```
Class.forName("sun.jdbc.odbc.JdbcOdbcDriver");
```

To load a different JDBC DBMS driver, see your driver documentation for the class name to use.

The following example application loads several JDBC drivers. It then interrogates the `DriverManager` for a list of the registered drivers that are subsequently printed out. Some JDBC drivers are needed to make the examples in this unit work. When installing DB2 you will find the DB2 JDBC drivers in the installed directories. Add the location and name of the `db2java.zip` file in your CLASSPATH environment variable.

```
import java.sql.*;

class DrvLister {

  public static void main(String argv[]) {
    try {
      Class.forName("com.ibm.db2.jdbc.app.DB2Driver");
      Class.forName("com.ibm.db2.jdbc.net.DB2Driver");
      Class.forName("sun.jdbc.odbc.JdbcOdbcDriver");
    } catch (Exception e) {
      e.printStackTrace();
    }
    System.out.println("JDBC drivers loaded:");
    java.util.Enumeration enu = DriverManager.getDrivers();
    while(enu.hasMoreElements())
    System.out.println(enu.nextElement());
  }
}
```

Note: Loading a driver does not make it automatically available. A driver may have external dependencies and may check for certain conditions before registering itself with the `DriverManager`.

Connecting to Databases

In order to connect to a database, request a connection with the static method `DriverManager.getConnection()`. This is an overloaded function with three different signatures.

```
DriverManager.getConnection(String url)
DriverManager.getConnection(String url, String user, String
   password)
DriverManager.getConnection(String url, Properties info)
```

In each of the three implementations, the first parameter is a database connection URL. The second method accepts a user name and password required for an authenticated connection. The last method uses a `Property` object to send multiple parameters to the driver. The `Property` class inherits from the `Hashtable` class. It is used to save parameter names (the keys) and values.

The database connection URL specifies the target database and its location. It can also provide information to help the driver set the desired database connection characteristics when possible (for example, cache size). The format of the database connection URL is:

```
jdbc:<subprotocol>:<subname>
```

The *subprotocol* field is the name of the driver or database connectivity mechanism. For example, if you are using the JDBC-ODBC bridge driver, the JDBC URL subprotocol field will be `odbc`.

The *subname* field varies with the subprotocol that is used but is generally a logical name that is mapped by the database engine to a physical directory where the database tables are stored.

The driver manager receives the connection URL and passes it to all the loaded drivers. The first driver that accepts the URL as a valid connection string is used to connect to the database. If no driver accepts the URL, an `SQLException` exception (no suitable driver) is thrown.

When the connection is successfully established, a `Connection` object is returned by a call to `DriverManager.getConnection()`. A `Connection` object is responsible for transaction control. The transaction control methods that the `Connection` method implements are `commit()`, `rollback()`, and `setAutoCommit()`. The default behavior is to commit changes after each statement that is executed. The behavior can be changed by calling `setAutoCommit(false)` on the desired `Connection` object. The `Connection` object also provides information about the tables and stored procedures in the destination database and about the connection itself. The `getMetaData()` method describes all the information that a `Connection` object can provide.

Executing SQL Statements

Before executing an SQL statement, an application or an applet must call a method on the `Connection` object to obtain the correct `Statement` object. A

Table 9–1 JDBC Statement Objects

Return Object Type	Method	Description
Statement	createStatement()	Executes regular SQL expressions, such as SELECT, INSERT, DELETE, and DDL
PreparedStatement	prepareStatement()	Executes precompiled SQL statements
CallableStatement	prepareCall()	Makes calls to stored procedures

Statement object executes an SQL statement and obtains the results produced by it. Table 9–1 describes the three methods that return an object of a particular Statement type.

A discussion of stored procedures is beyond the scope of this book; thus, the CallableStatement class will neither be presented in the examples nor discussed further.

Two methods are provided by both Statement and PreparedStatement to execute SQL statements. The executeUpdate(String sql) method receives an SQL string containing an INSERT, DELETE, or UPDATE statement and returns the number of rows updated. This method is also used to execute DDL statements. The executeQuery(String sql) method runs a SELECT statement against the database. This method returns a ResultSet object containing the resultant rows from the database query.

Using the PreparedStatement Class

Precompiled SQL statements are statements defined at compile time (in the source code) with values that can be set at runtime. An example of a precompiled statement is:

```
SELECT * FROM pepper WHERE heatlevel = ?
```

The question mark can be replaced with the desired value at runtime, but the statement is fixed in the code.

The PreparedStatement class provides all the necessary methods to set values in a precompiled statement with the correct SQL type. Consult the JDBC API documentation for all the data type conversion methods. Some of the more common methods used to set the parameter value with the correct SQL data type are listed below.

- `setBoolean()`
- `setDate()`
- `setFloat()`
- `setInt()`
- `setNull()`
- `setObject()`
- `setString()`

The following code snippet demonstrates how to execute a precompiled SQL statement.

```
. . .
PreparedStatement statement = connection.prepareStatement(
    "UPDATE peppers SET heatLevel = ? WHERE kind = ?");
statement.setInt(1, 10);
statement.setString(2, "Bell");
int updatedRows = statement.executeUpdate();
. . .
```

Using the Statement Class

Statement objects are used to send a string containing an SQL statement to the database.

The following code snippet demonstrates how to execute a regular SQL statement.

```
. . .
Statement statement = connection.createStatement();
ResultSet rows = statement.executeQuery("SELECT * FROM
  peppers");
. . .
```

Using Database Literals

The JDBC specification defines the use of database literals. JDBC follows the ISO standard format. Table 9–2 shows the supported database literals and their format.

Table 9–2 JDBC Supported Database Literals

Type	Literal
Date	{d 'yyyy-mm-dd'}
Time	{t 'hh:mm:ss'}
Timestamp	{ts 'yyyy-mm-dd hh:mm:ss.f...'}

Reading Query Results

The executeQuery() method returns the selected rows in a ResultSet object. The selected rows are sequentially accessible with the aid of the next() method. The first call of the next() method makes the first row the current row in the ResultSet object.

The columns in the current row can be retrieved by number or by name. Retrieving columns by number is more efficient than retrieving columns by name; however, it is less flexible. Column indices start at 1.

The ResultSet class provides a complete set of *get* methods to read column contents. These methods try to convert the SQL type to the desired Java type. Consult the JDBC API documentation for all the datatype conversion methods. Some of the more common methods used to read the contents of a column are listed below.

- getBoolean(int)
  getBoolean(String)

- getDate(int)
  getDate(String)

- getFloat(int)
  getFloat(String)

- getInt(int)
  getInt(String)

- getString(int)
  getString(String)

The ResultSet class also provides the wasNull() method to determine whether the last column read was an SQL null value. The get methods always return a compatible Java value for SQL null values: null for objects, 0 for numeric values, and false for boolean values.

Table 9–3 The Pepper Database Table

Code	Kind	Heat Level	Price
0	Habanero	300000	1.45
1	Serrano	10000	1.25
2	Jalapeno	5000	0.99
3	Bell	0	0.75

JDBC Example

The following example assumes that the Pepper table (Table 9–3) is created, popu-lated, and exists in a PEPPER database.

The example application issues an SQL SELECT statement and prints the result data to the screen.

```
import java.net.URL;
import java.sql.*;

class DbApp {
  private final int ALIGNLEFT  = 0;
  private final int ALIGNRIGHT = 1;
  private Statement stmt;
  private ResultSet rs;

  public static void main(String argv[]) {
    DbApp db = new DbApp();
  }
```

The class DbApp contains variables for the statement and the result set. The int instance variables align the display of results of queries on the database. The main() method starts the example application by creating a new instance of DbApp.

```
  public DbApp() {
    try {
      // Register the driver
      Class.forName("com.ibm.db2.jdbc.app.DB2Driver");
      connectDB();
      runQuery("SELECT kind,heatlevel,price FROM pepper");
      displayData();
```

```
      stmt.close();
   } catch (Exception e) {
      e.printStackTrace();
   }
}
```

The constructor registers the DB2 driver and connects to the database. A query is run on the database to select the kind, heat level, and price properties for each pepper in the Pepper table.

```
private void connectDB() throws SQLException {
   // Prepare the connection URL
   String db   = "PEPPER";
   String url = "jdbc:db2:" + db;
   // Set the user and password
   String userid = "mkomis";
   String password = "ncc";
   System.out.println("Connecting to the DB");
   Connection con = DriverManager.getConnection(url,
userid, password);
   stmt = con.createStatement();
}
```

The userid and password variables may need to be changed to match the values defined in your system.

The connectDB() method establishes a connection to the sample database. An SQLException is generated if the connection cannot be established. The URL of the database, the user ID, and the password are sent to the DriverManager to establish the connection. The createStatement() method returns an instance of Statement that can be used to execute regular SQL expressions like SELECT, INSERT, DELETE, and DDL. The Statement object is assigned to the stmt instance variable.

```
private void runQuery(String aSQLStatement) throws SQLException {
   System.out.println("Running the query: " + aSQLStatement +
"\n");
   rs = stmt.executeQuery(aSQLStatement);
}
```

The runQuery() method accepts a String representation of an SQL statement and passes it to the Statement object obtained earlier to execute against the database. The ResultSet object that is returned is assigned to instance variable rs. If the query cannot be executed, an SQLException is generated. A line listing the SQL statement is written to the console.

```
private void displayData() throws SQLException {
  System.out.println("Kind      Level  $/lb");
  System.out.println("-------- ------ -----");
  while (rs.next()) {
    String kind  = rs.getString("kind");
    String level = rs.getString("heatlevel");
    String price = rs.getString("price");
    System.out.print(padString(kind, 8, ALIGNLEFT) + " ");
    System.out.print(padString(level, 6, ALIGNRIGHT) + " ");
    System.out.println(padString(price, 5, ALIGNRIGHT) + " ");
  }
}
```

The displayData() method displays the data contained in the result set of the last query on the console. The int variables defined at the beginning are used to size and adjust the display. The individual strings are accessed from the result set by using getString() and passing the name of the variable as the key.

```
private String padString(String aString, int aLength,
      int anAlignment) {
  if (aString.length() == aLength) {
    return aString;
  } else if (aString.length() > aLength) {
    return aString.substring(0, aLength);
  } else {
    char[] dstArray = new char[aLength];
    if (anAlignment == ALIGNLEFT) {
      aString.getChars(0, aString.length(), dstArray, 0);
    } else if (anAlignment == ALIGNRIGHT)
      aString.getChars(0, aString.length(),
        dstArray, aLength - aString.length());
    return new String(dstArray);
  }
}
```

The padString() method uses blanks to pad a String to a desired length in the direction specified. The getChars() method copies characters from a string, starting at the position specified, into the destination character array starting at the position specified.

When run, the example program should output the following result.

```
Connecting to the DB
Running the query: SELECT kind,heatlevel,price FROM pepper

Kind        Level  $/lb
--------    ------  -----
Habanero 300000   1.45
Serrano   10000   1.25
Jalapeno   5000   0.99
Bell           0   0.75
```

Java Transactions

In enterprise computing, transaction processing is critical for businesses that require reliable, efficient, and manageable computing solutions. Many of the concepts used in today's distributed and fault-tolerant systems are the result of transaction processing systems that introduced the concept of a transaction.

Distributed transaction processing is one of the most notable features of EJB. Enterprise Java Beans participating in a transaction can seamlessly update data in multiple databases across multiple locations. Generally, a programmer of an Enterprise Java Bean or EJB client does not need to code transaction logic because the container and EJB server providers bear the responsibility for managing transactions. Any Enterprise Java Bean participating in a transaction can also initiate multiple transactions across multiple EJB servers. The process of propagating the transaction context across each server is totally transparent to an Enterprise Java Bean or an EJB client programmer.

Each Enterprise Java Bean has an associated transaction attribute that can be modified by tools that come with an EJB server or the EJB development software. The possible values of the attribute are as follows.

- TX_NOT_SUPPORTED — Indicates that the Bean does not support transactions. Any method invocation on the Bean should occur outside the scope of a transaction. If a transaction is currently in progress, it is suspended until the method completes.

- TX_BEAN_MANAGED — Provides a mechanism for a Bean to programmatically demarcate transaction boundaries. The Bean uses the UserTransaction interface (see below).

- TX_REQUIRED — Any invocation of a method on the Bean must execute within the context of a transaction. The method call uses the client's transaction context if there is one; otherwise, a new transaction is started by the container.

- `TX_SUPPORTS` — The Bean supports, but doesn't require, a transaction context. Any method call on the Bean uses the client's transaction context if there is one; otherwise, no transaction context is used.

- `TX_REQUIRES_NEW` — A new transaction context is always created for the Bean. If a transaction is currently in progress, it is suspended until the new transaction completes.

- `TX_MANDATORY` — The Bean must execute within an existing client transaction context. Any method call on the Bean uses the client's transaction context if there is one; otherwise, a `TransactionRequired` exception is thrown.

In the cases that an Enterprise Java Bean or EJB client wants to control the transaction boundaries explicitly, the EJB architecture provides the means that make such control possible. But first, here is an overview of the transaction management facilities that are provided by Java. At the time of this writing, there are two Java packages related to transaction management.

- **JTS (Java Transaction Service)** — A low-level transaction management specification consisting of the standard Java mapping of the OMG Object Transaction Service.

- **JTA (Java Transaction API)** — A high-level transaction management specification consisting of two components:

  - `javax.transaction.UserTransaction` – A simple application transaction demarcation interface

  - `javax.transaction.xa` – The Java mapping of the X/Open XA API

An EJB client developer wishing to programmatically control the transaction boundaries can use the `javax.transaction.UserTransaction` interface directly. For an Enterprise JavaBean developer needing programmatic transaction control, the transaction attribute associated with the Bean should be set to `TX_BEAN_MANAGED`, and the `javax.transaction.UserTransaction` interface can be obtained through the `EJBContext.getUserTransaction()` method, as demonstrated in the following snippet of code.

```
import javax.transaction.UserTransaction;
...
EJBContext ic = ...;
...
try {
  UserTransaction tx = ic.getUserTransaction();
} catch (IllegalStateException e) {
```

```
   // Transaction attribute not set to TX_BEAN_MANAGED
   ...
}
...
tx.begin();
    // code within scope of transaction goes here
tx.commit();
```

Java Naming and Directory Interface (JNDI)

Within any networked system, naming and directory facilities are essential in finding the required resources, whether they are users, computers, applications, or Beans. Java Naming and Directory Interface (JNDI) is a Java API that provides naming and directory services to classes written in Java. The API allows the storage and retrieval of the name of any Java object. Attributes can be associated with the name, and facilities are provided to search for objects by attributes.

The JNDI API is independent of physical implementation, and so it provides a common interface to one or more naming services. Different services provided can be seamlessly made available behind the API. Therefore, existing directories implemented in directories, such as LDAP, NDS, DNS, and NIS(YP), can be used by Java applications, thus simplifying the integration of Java applications with existing systems. An interface is also defined for service providers, to enable their directory or naming service through JNDI.

The JNDI API is packaged in `javax.naming` for the naming interface and `javax.naming.directory` for the directory interface. Let's now look at these interfaces in more detail.

The Naming Interface

All the basic operations of adding a name to object binding, looking up an object, listing all the binding, and removing binding is provided by the core service— `javax.naming.Context`. In addition, binding can be grouped into contexts and services that are provided to create and delete them.

The most commonly used operation is likely to be `Context.lookup()`. This method returns an object of the class appropriate to the application. For example, if an application wanted to find a particular customer, Mr. Big, it could be coded:

```
Customer mrBig = (Customer) ctx.lookup("Mr.Big");
```

In this way, the programmer is not aware of the naming service that will find Mr. Big. A new naming service could be added to the system, and the application would not be aware of it or impacted if it was running.

The Directory Interface

The directory interface is implemented as `DirContext`. This interface provides methods to examine and update the attributes associated with a directory object. The `Attribute` class has a string identifier and any number of values of any type. The directory object contains any number of `Attribute` objects.

`DirContext` extends the `Context` interface and, therefore, also behaves as a naming context. This means that a context could logically have all the directory entries and the bindings within it.

The `DirContext` interface also supports searching of the directory content. For example, given a list of attributes, some with specific values to find, the `DirContext.search()` method will return the matching directory objects.

JNDI Example

An EJB client uses the JNDI API to locate an EJB's home interface. After finding a home interface, a client can find or create an instance of the EJB. Code similar to the following example code snippets is used in the samples in this book to locate an EJB's home interface.

The client's first step is to use the JNDI name services to locate a name server. This step involves creating an initial context. In the following code snippet, we indicate that we intend to use the `CosNaming` initial context factory to create an initial context. We also indicate, by specifying a provider URL of `"iiop:///"`, that the name server is on the local host and listening on the default port.

```
// Get the initial context
java.util.Hashtable properties = new java.util.Hashtable(2);
// local name server
properties.put(javax.naming.Context.PROVIDER_URL, "iiop:///");
   properties.put(javax.naming.Context.INITIAL_CONTEXT_FACTORY,
        "com.ibm.jndi CosNaming.CNInitialContextFactory");
javax.naming.InitialContext initContext = new
                  javax.naming.InitialContext(properties);
```

The next step is to look up the required object. In the case of an EJB client, this object will be an EJB's home interface. The following is a snippet taken from Sample 1 in this book. See "Putting the Theory to Work" on page 141. The `SimpleCustomer` EJB of Sample 1 was configured with a JNDI home name of `SimpleCustomer`. Because we are using CORBA's `CosNaming`, a CORBA object is returned by the `lookup()` method; the object is subsequently narrowed to be of type `SimpleCustomerHome` (Note: A Java typecast cannot be used in the place of a CORBA narrow for CORBA objects).

```
// Perform the lookup
SimpleCustomerHome simpleCustomerHome = null;

Object obj = initContext.lookup("SimpleCustomer"); // the JNDI name
if (obj instanceof org.omg.CORBA.Object)
{
    simpleCustomerHome =
  SimpleCustomerHomeHelper.narrow((org.omg.CORBA.Object) obj);
}
else {
System.out.println("Lookup returned unexpected object type.");
    System.exit(0);
}
```

Remote Method Invocation (RMI)

Java Remote Method Invocation (RMI) allows you to write distributed applications, using pure Java. RMI provides a simple and direct model for distributed
interactions between Java objects. These objects can be new Java objects, which
are written to use RMI directly, or they can be simple Java wrappers around existing software components and APIs. Because RMI is centered around Java, it
brings the Java safety and portability to distributed computing. Applications can
be easily partitioned and distributed across a network of servers to best fit enterprise requirements.

This section does not provide a complete description of all the details about RMI.
Instead, it gives you a broad overview of the technology and illustrates its simplicity and power. Please refer to the JavaSoft documentation
(http://java.sun.com/products/jdk/rmi) for details and the latest
updates about RMI. There, you will also find a number of tutorials on how to
use RMI.

Typical RMI applications often comprise two or more separate programs: a client
and one or more servers. A server application usually creates a number of remote
objects, makes the references to those objects accessible to the clients, and waits
for clients to invoke methods on the remote objects. A classic client application
first gets remote references to one or more remote objects on the server and then
invokes methods on them. RMI provides the mechanism by which the client and
the server communicate and pass information back and forth. Such an application
is sometimes referred to as a distributed object application because it allows both
the client, as well as the server, to be any Java object.

Some RMI Highlights

The following paragraphs list the most important features of RMI. Note that this
list is neither all-inclusive nor descriptive of all feature functionality.

Simplified Writing of Reliable Distributed Applications

RMI simplifies the development of remote Java servers and Java clients that access those servers. A remote object is accessed from a client by its remote interface, which is an actual Java interface. A server-side object needs roughly three lines of code to declare itself a server object; otherwise, it is like any other Java object. This simplicity makes it easy to quickly write servers for full-scale distributed object systems and to rapidly develop prototypes and early versions of software for testing and evaluation.

Seamless Remote Method Invocation

RMI enables seamless and natural invocation of methods on objects in different Java virtual machines (JVMs) by providing location transparency. Once a reference to a remote object has been obtained, the client application calling a method of a remote object is unaware of the location of the remote object. The remote object can run in a remote JVM, or it can run in the same JVM as the client.

For a client, calling a method on a remote object is no different from calling a method on a local object. That is, there is no need to deploy code for remote objects to the client prior to using these objects. The JVM and the RMI subsystems provide the means to transparently load the client interface of remote objects on a just-in-time basis.

RMI integrates the distributed object model into the Java language in a natural way while retaining most of the Java language's object semantics and type-safety provided by the Java runtime environment.

Parameter Passing "By Value"

RMI lets you ship objects directly across connections with no extra client code needed. It can pass copies of full objects as arguments from the client to the server and return objects back to the client as method return values. Any complex object—not just predefined flat data types, as is the case with RPC or CORBA 2.1— can be passed by value as a single argument. This means that composite objects (objects that refer internally to other objects, for example, a hash table holding references to multiple elements) are completely resolved, serialized, and passed over the connection, where they are reinflated to the original structure.

Remote objects can also be passed back and forth between the client and the server. However, remote objects are never passed by value. They are always passed by reference, thereby ensuring remote object identity and uniqueness in a distributed environment.

Local Execution and Central Code Management

With RMI, you can have the client upload behavior from the server with a simple method invocation. This provides a flexible way of off-loading computation from the server to the clients while still maintaining a centralized code base.

When a client application needs to run a certain business function, the client asks the server for a Java object that implements the function's interface. If this is the first time that the client's RMI runtime has seen a reference to this particular function implementation, RMI will ask the server for a copy of the object implementing the function. Should the application require the same function again, the RMI runtime will provide the object uploaded beforehand without going back to the server. If the implementation of the function changes tomorrow, the RMI runtime will then upload that new implementation of the business function interface.

Note: It is equally possible to use this mechanism the other way around; that is, the server downloads Java objects that implement a specific functionality from the client for execution, thus providing the execution environment for arbitrary client tasks.

Safe Java Environment

There are clear safety and security implications when you are executing RMI requests. RMI provides for secure channels between client and server and the isolation of downloaded implementations inside a security Sandbox to protect your system from possible attacks by untrusted clients.

RMI uses the built-in Java security mechanisms that allow your system to be safe when users download object implementations. RMI uses the security manager to protect systems and networks from potentially downloading and executing hostile code. RMI further provides a feature called custom RMI socket factory that allows RMI clients and servers to talk across sockets that implement special qualities, such as encryption or compression.

Connectivity to Non-Java Applications

RMI client/server applications can connect to existing server applications and legacy systems by means of the standard Java Native method Interface (JNI) to provide for bridging. JNI allows Java applications to directly call functions written in other languages, such as C and C++. Using RMI and JNI, you can write your client in Java and use your existing implementation of a server. RMI can also connect to existing relational databases, using the standard JDBC package. The RMI/JNI and RMI/JDBC combinations let you use RMI to communicate with existing servers in non-Java languages and to expand your use of Java to those servers.

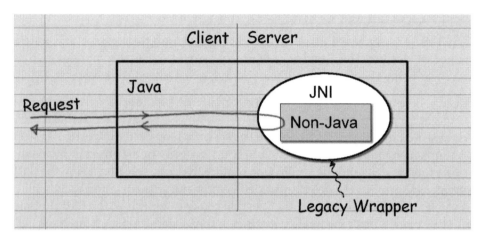

Figure 9–2   *Java-to-Legacy Bridging with JNI*

Figure 9–2 illustrates bridging, using a small legacy wrapper function that encapsulates the existing legacy API written in a non-Java language.

Full Core-Java Integration

RMI is part of the core Java platform starting with JDK 1.1, so it exists on every Java virtual machine supporting JDK 1.1 or higher. This implies that any RMI-based system is 100 percent portable to any JVM 1.1 or higher. All RMI systems talk the same public protocol, so all Java systems can talk directly to each other without any protocol translation overhead.

RMI is multithreaded, allowing your servers to exploit Java threads for concurrent processing of client requests. RMI uses distributed garbage collection to collect remote server objects that are no longer referenced by any clients in the network. Analogous to garbage collection inside a Java virtual machine, distributed garbage collection allows you to create server objects as needed knowing that they will be removed when they no longer need to be accessible to clients.

Bridging to CORBA IIOP

The implementation of the Java RMI interface on top of the CORBA IIOP protocol combines two strong distributed object technologies. RMI over IIOP allows Java objects to interoperate directly with CORBA objects over the CORBA IIOP wire protocol. However, this statement does not imply that the full set of RMI services will be available over IIOP (at least not at the time of this writing)—CORBA interfaces are subject to the CORBA Interface Definition Language (IDL) specification that currently (CORBA 2.1) does not include definitions for pass-by-value capabilities and other RMI-specific features.

However, JavaSoft is working with OMG to extend the IIOP specification to accommodate more functionality, thereby increasing the level of integration between the two technologies. JavaSoft claims, "In the future the Java specification will be extended to define a standard interface for accessing CORBA IDL services using RMI-style API and semantics."

Remote Object Activation

Remote Object Activation is a new feature introduced with JDK 1.2. It allows servers to create remote objects on demand rather than creating and registering them at server startup, thus saving resources. It allows clients to hold references to persistent remote objects without requiring that those objects remain executing in a runtime environment at all times.

How RMI Works

The following list shows the various actions involved in a remote method invocation.

1. **Locate remote objects.**

   Client applications can use one of two mechanisms to obtain a reference to a remote object. A server application can register its remote object with RMI's simple naming facility, the *rmiregistry*, allowing the client to request the remote object reference from the naming service. Alternatively, the server application can return remote object references as part of normal method return values.

2. **Communicate with remote objects.**

   The details of communication between local and remote objects are handled transparently by RMI. To the programmer, remote communication looks like a standard Java method invocation. RMI takes care of parameter and return value passing and the like.

3. **Load classes for objects that are passed as parameters or return values.**

   Recall that RMI allows a caller to pass instances of any Java class as arguments to a remote method call, including composite objects, and the remote objects method can return objects of any class as return value. For this reason, it is quite likely that the remote or local virtual machine or both may receive embedded objects for which they do not have corresponding class files accessible. RMI provides the necessary mechanisms for loading an object's class if it cannot be found in the local set of classes (referenced by the CLASSPATH variable).

A Simple Example

Figure 9–3 depicts an RMI distributed application that uses the registry to obtain a reference to a remote object. The server calls the registry to associate a name with a remote object. The client looks up the remote object by its name in the server's registry and eventually invokes a method on it. Figure 9–3 also shows that the RMI system can use an existing Web server to load Java classes for objects, when needed, in both directions—from server to client and from client to server.

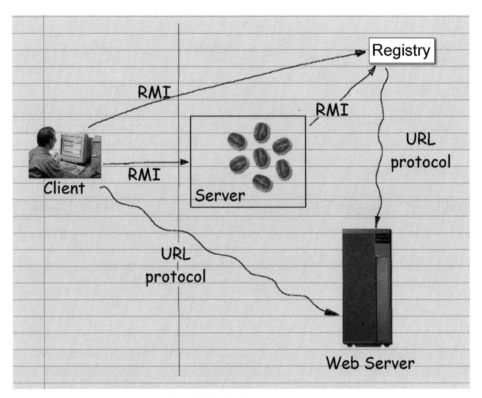

Figure 9–3 *Explaining the RMI Mechanism*

The following subsections briefly explain the various elements involved in RMI.

The Remote Interface

The remote interface defines the set of business methods that can be called by a client on a remote object. The remote interface is a Java interface class used by the client to interact with the remote object.

Note: The remote interface does not have to include all public methods that the server class implements.

The following code snippet illustrates a possible remote interface for a bank account remote object class.

```
public interface BankAccount extends java.rmi.Remote {
    public void deposit(float amount) throws
  java.rmi.RemoteException;
    public void withdraw(float amount)
        throws OverdrawnException, java.rmi.RemoteException;
}
```

The Remote Object Class

The remote object class is the class that implements the server-side business functionality, that is, at least the set of methods defined in the remote interface. The remote object class can implement other methods not declared in the interface and, therefore, not accessible to remote clients.

The code section below shows how a remote object class might implement the remote interface defined above.

```
public class BankAccountImpl extends UnicastRemoteObject
    implements BankAccount
{
    // constructor(s) and a destructor come here...
    ...
    public void deposit(float amount) throws RemoteException {
        // implementation of deposit()...
    }
    public void withdraw(float amount) throws
  RemoteException,
        OverdrawnException {
        // implementation of withdraw()...
    }
}
```

Stubs and Skeletons

RMI uses a standard mechanism for communicating with remote objects: stubs and skeletons.

A stub for a remote object acts as a client's local representative (also called proxy) for the remote object. The client effectively invokes a method on the local stub, thinking it would talk directly to the remote object. The stub connects to the remote objects JVM, passes the method call and all the parameters, and waits for the remote method to return, possibly producing a result that is transferred back to the client. A stub for a remote object implements the same remote interface that its remote object implements.

In JDK 1.1, the remote VM uses a skeleton object as a counterpart to the client-side stub. The skeleton handles the method identification and the parameters sent by the stub and invokes the (local) call to the appropriate method of the remote object implementation. It then passes back the return value to the client-side stub.

In JDK1.2, an additional stub protocol was introduced that eliminates the need for skeletons. Instead, generic code is used to carry out the duties performed by skeletons in JDK1.1.

Stubs and skeletons are generated by a tool called the rmic compiler, which is part of the JDK.

The RMI Bootstrap Registry

For a client to invoke a method on a remote object, that client must first obtain a reference to the object. The RMI system provides a simple bootstrap name server, called the RMI bootstrap registry, from which a client can obtain remote objects on a given host. The bootstrap registry provides methods to look up remote object references from a Uniform Resource Locator (URL).

For a client to be able to find a remote object reference in the bootstrap registry, the server must register the remote object and provide a remote object name (an alias) for the client to identify the remote object.

The following line of code illustrates how a server might register a remote object by using the java.rmi.Naming class.

```
Naming.rebind("//<host-name>/MyBankAccount",
              new BankAccountImpl());
```

Of course, in a real application, a server should rather register a remote object implementing a bank that would provide some account lookup methods that return references to bank account objects instead of registering each individual bank account with the naming service.

Also, note that the registry is not persistent, meaning that all remote object references in the registry are lost if the server shuts down or crashes. The server application must register all remote objects at server startup.

Local Objects

The local object designates the client-side object that invokes method calls on remote objects. A local object must first obtain a reference to the remote object by requesting the reference from the RMI bootstrap registry. It can then issue a method call on the remote object proxy it receives from the RMI subsystem.

Here's a code snippet illustrating the lookup procedure and method call to a remote bank account object.

```
BankAccount account = null;
try {
    account = (BankAccount)Naming.lookup(
        "//" + getCodeBase().getHost() + "/MyBankAccount");
    account.deposit(200.0);
} catch (Exception e) {
    // lookup failed, do exception handling here...
}
```

The `java.rmi.Naming` class encapsulates the calls to the remote RMI bootstrap server to look up the remote object.

Servlets

Servlets are programs written in Java that run on a server. The concept of a servlet running on a server is analogous to an applet running on a client. Servlets can be used to dynamically extend server-side functionality. For example, an HTTP servlet running on an HTTP server can be used to generate dynamic HTML content.

Servlets are most widely used on HTTP servers. HTTP servlets are an effective replacement for CGI (Common Gateway Interface) scripts. CGI scripts are typically written in languages such as Perl, C, or C++. Unlike CGI scripts, which are often platform specific, servlets are inherently platform independent because they are written in Java and developed with the Java Servlet API. Servlets generally offer better performance than their CGI counterparts and are typically easier to write.

Servlet Architecture

The Java Servlet API comes in two packages: `javax.servlet`, the protocol independent part of the API; and `javax.servlet.http`, the HTTP-specific part of the API.

All servlets implement the `javax.servlet.Servlet` interface, although most servlets don't implement this interface directly but rather extend classes that implement the `Servlet` interface. Two abstract classes provided by the Java Servlet API implement the `Servlet` interface: `GenericServlet`, used for writing protocol-independent servlets, and `HttpServlet`, used for writting HTTP servlets.

Servlet Life Cycle

The following methods declared in the `Servlet` interface represent the milestones of a servlet life cycle.

- `init()` — Initializes the servlet.

  The `init()` method is called only once, at the beginning of the servlet life cycle when the servlet is loaded by the server. The `init()` method is useful for writing code, such as initializing database connections or calling other initializing methods that might manage costly resources for the lifetime of the servlet. If a servlet has no special servlet initialization needs, then the default implementation of the `init()` method (as provided by either `GenericServlet` or `HttpServlet`) should be sufficient.

- `service()` — Handles every client request.

  The `service()` method is the heart of a servlet and is called for every client request. When a servlet accepts a request from a client, the `service()` method is passed two parameters, a request and response object that are the means by which a servlet communicates with the server and, ultimately, with the client. The default `service()` method implementation provided by the `HttpServlet` abstract class is rarely overridden for HTTP servlets.

- `destroy()` — Performs final cleanup in preparation for unloading.

  The `destroy()` method is used for special cleanup needs. It is called when a server is ready to unload the servlet. Like the `init()` method, it is only called once. Typical use of the method is for writing code that closes active connections or releases resources. If a servlet has no special cleanup needs, then the default implementation of the `destroy()` method (as provided by either `GenericServlet` or `HttpServlet`) should be sufficient.

The `GenericServlet` and `HttpServlet` abstract classes provide default implementations of the life-cycle methods.

Servlet Request and Response Objects

Recall that when a servlet accepts a request from a client, the `service()` method is passed two objects of the following types as parameters.

- `ServletRequest` — Provides methods for a servlet to access request parameters, request headers, and CGI-like environment variables of an incoming client request. Also allows a servlet to access a `ServletInputStream` (an extension of the `InputStream` interface) for reading binary data or a `BufferedReader` for reading text from the client request.

- `ServletResponse` — Provides methods to send the response that a servlet has prepared back to the client. It provides access to a `ServletOutput-Stream` (an extension of the `OutputStream` interface) for writing binary data responses or a `PrintWriter` for writing formatted text responses.

Additional HTTP-specific support is provided by the `HttpServletRequest` interface, which extends `ServletRequest`, and the `HttpServletResponse` interface, which extends `ServletResponse`.

Writing Servlets

As servlets are most widely used on HTTP servers, the following discussion on writting servlets will concentrate on HTTP servlets. HTTP servlets are written by subclassing the `HttpServlet` class. Because the class is abstract, servlet writers must override at least one method. The methods that are normally overridden are:

- `doGet(HttpServletRequest, HttpServletResponse)` — For handling HTTP GET, conditional GET, and HEAD requests.

- `doPost(HttpServletRequest, HttpServletResponse)` — For handling HTTP POST requests.

- `doPut(HttpServletRequest, HttpServletResponse)` — For handling HTTP PUT requests.

- `doDelete(HttpServletRequest, HttpServletResponse)` — For handling HTTP DELETE requests.

- The servlet life-cycle milestone methods `init()` and `destroy()` — Only if the servlet writer has some special initialization or destruction needs.

The `service()` method, as implemented by the `HttpServlet` class, supports standard HTTP requests that are dispatched to appropriate methods, for example, the GET, POST, and PUT requests are dispatched to the `doGet()`, `doPost()`, and `doPut()` methods. The HTTP OPTIONS and TRACE requests are automatically handled, as the `HttpServlet` class provides suitable implementations for the corresponding `doOptions()` and `doTrace()` methods.

By subclassing `HttpServlet` class and implementing the `doGet()` method, a servlet automatically supports the HTTP requests GET, HEAD, and conditional GET. Implementing the `getLastModified()` method enables caching, thus improving Web server performance. Servlets are typically singletons, meaning that a single instance of the servlet is created to handle multiple client requests. Since these requests could be concurrent, servlets must be written to handle simultaneous requests and multithreading. Access to shared resources, such as class variables and in-memory data, must be synchronized or the servlet is not thread safe and may not run properly.

When the HTTP server calls the `service()` method of a servlet, it passes request and response objects as parameters. The `HttpServletRequest` and `HttpServletResponse` objects are the way in which the servlet communicates with the server and, ultimately, with the client.

The methods from the `HttpServletRequest` object obtain information about the client environment, the server environment, and any information provided by the client (for example, form information set by GET or POST). The methods used to retrieve these pieces of information are `getParameterNames()`, `getParameter()`, `getParameterValues()`, and `getQueryString()`.

The HTTP servlet invokes the `HttpServletResponse` methods to send the response that it has prepared back to the client. Its methods allow the response header and the response body to be set (for example, `setContentType()` sets the content type of the response). The response object also has the `getWriter()` method to return a `PrintWriter` object for writing formatted text responses.

A sample `HelloWorld` servlet follows.

```
public class HelloWorldServlet extends HttpServlet
{
  public void doGet (HttpServletRequest request,
                     HttpServletResponse response)
  throws ServletException, IOException
  {
    response.setContentType("text/html");
    PrintWriter out = response.getWriter();
    out.println("<HTML><HEAD><TITLE>");
    out.println("HelloworldServlet Example");
    out.println("</TITLE></HEAD><BODY>");
    out.println("<P>Hello World!");
    out.println("</BODY></HTML>");
    out.close();
  }
}
```

JavaServer Pages

JavaServer Pages (JSP) provides a simple, but powerful, solution that allows dynamic HTML generation on a Web server. JSP is similar in concept to other Web server-side environments, such as Microsoft Active Server Pages (ASP) and Netscape Server-Side JavaScript (SSJS).

JSP simplifies the creation and management of dynamic content by clearly separating content generation (business logic programing) from content presentation (HTML coding). The business logic for content generation resides in reusable components. Examples include servlets, Java Beans, and Enterprise Java Beans. JSP also supports embedding Java code used for scripting within Web pages.

JavaServer Pages (.jsp) files contain combinations of HTML tags, National Center for Supercomputing Applications (NCSA) tags, and JSP syntax.

Access to JavaServer Pages

When a Web server receives a request for a JavaServer Pages (.jsp) file for the first time, the Web server parses the .jsp file and generates Java source code for a servlet. The servlet's code is then compiled and executed to generate HTML pages with dynamic content.

The compiled servlet is stored in memory on the server and reused for subsequent requests of the .jsp file. An exception is made if the server detects that the .jsp file has changed, in which case, the servlet is regenerated and stored in memory on the server. Below, we discuss the two alternative models for .jsp file access.

The first access model involves a Web browser making a direct request to a .jsp file, as shown in Figure 9–4.

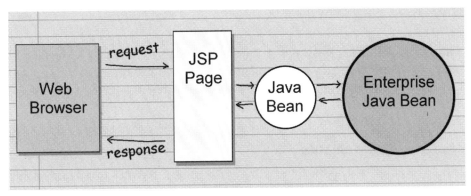

Figure 9–4 *Direct Request by Client for a JSP Page*

After the request is made by the client, the .jsp file makes a request to a Java Bean that performs a particular computation, and the results are written in the Java Bean's properties. The .jsp file then reads the properties of the Java Bean to generate the HTML dynamic content and then presents it to the client. In this example, the dynamic content generation is by means of a Java Bean interrogating an Enterprise Java Bean.

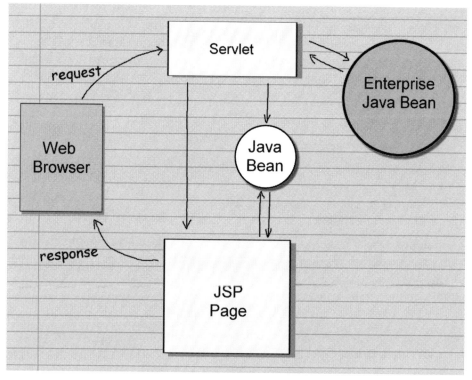

Figure 9–5 *Indirect Request by a Client for a JSP Page*

An alternative model of sending a request to a JSP page is for a Java servlet to handle the client request, as shown in Figure 9–5. A request comes in to a servlet, which generates the dynamic content and writes the dynamic content into the properties of a Java Bean. The Java Bean is used by the .jsp file to access the dynamic contents and then to present the file to the client as HTML.

JavaServer Pages Syntax

It should be noted that, at the time of this writing, the JSP syntax was in a constant state of flux. Readers are encouraged to refer to any JSP documentation that accompanies their Web server for the required JSP syntax, as it may neither reflect the current JavaServer Pages specification from JavaSoft nor what is written here. This section discusses the syntax of a .jsp file as based on the 0.92 specification of JavaServer Pages.

HTML Tags

All the valid HTML tags are supported. For a description of these tags, refer to your favorite HTML Web programming reference.

NCSA Tags

JavaServer Pages supports server-side includes (SSI) directives based on the NCSA tag format. SSI provides the ability to embed a HTML file (or even a Java-Server Pages file) in the current HTML (or JavaServer Pages) file. For a description of the SSI directives, see your Web server's manual or one of the many books on Web programming.

JSP Syntax

JavaServer Pages can be divided into component-centric tags and scripting-centric tags. The component-centric tags facilitate the separation of business logic or programmatic content generation from content presentation. The business logic resides in Java Beans; the component-centric tags are the means by which .jsp files access the Java Beans and their properties.

Occasionally, it might be useful to embed small pieces of code directly in the .jsp files. Code embedding can be achieved by means of scripting-centric tags. Because scripting-centric tags aren't used too often, we simply summarize them in the next section, then look in-depth at the component-centric tags in a later section.

JavaServer Pages Scripting-Centric Tags

JSP scripting-centric tags consist of the following types.

- **Directives** (enclosed within < and >). The JSP directives include:

    - LANGUAGE – Scripting language being used (default is Java)

    - ERRORPAGE – Page to be returned if the current .jsp page results in an error

    - IMPORT – Packages the generated servlet imports

- **Declarations** (enclosed within <SCRIPT> and </SCRIPT>). Defines class-wide variables for the generated servlet class.

- **Scriptlets** (enclosed within <% and %>). A scriplet can consist of any valid Java code. A scriptlet's code is incorporated into the generated servlet's code.

- **Expressions** (enclosed within <%= and %>). A valid Java expression. The expression is evaluated, then its value is converted to a string, which is placed in the generated HTML dynamic content.

JavaServer Pages Component-Centric Tags

USEBEAN Tag

A USEBEAN tag declares the existence of a Java Bean in a `.jsp` file. The Bean and its properties can then be accessed later in the `.jsp` file. The syntax for a USEBEAN tag is:

```
<USEBEAN NAME = "bean instance name"
    TYPE = "bean class name"
    LIFESPAN="page|session|application">
```

and

```
</USEBEAN>
```

where the attributes are as follows.

- NAME — A name to declare a specific instance of a Bean. The name is case sensitive and must be unique within a `.jsp` file.

- TYPE — The name of the class that defines the Bean.

- LIFESPAN — The lifetime of the Bean, the valid values are:

  - page – The Bean is valid for the duration of the page request. If the Bean is not present in the page request, it is created and stored as part of the page request.

  - session – If the Bean is present in the current session, the Bean is reused. If the Bean is not present, it is created and stored as part of the HTTP session.

  - application – If the Bean is present in the current application, the Bean is reused. If the Bean is not present, it is created and stored as part of the application to which the `.jsp` file belongs.

The only valid tags that the opening `<USEBEAN...>` and closing `</USEBEAN>` tag pair can enclose are the following two tags.

- Zero or more occurrences of the `<SETONCREATE ...>` tag

- Zero or more occurrences of the `<SETFROMREQUEST ...>` tag

The SETONCREATE tag allows a Bean property named in the tag to be set to a specified value at the Bean's creation time. The syntax for a SETONCREATE tag is as follows.

```
<SETONCREATE
    BEANPROPERTY = "property name"
    VALUE = "property value">
```

A Bean property or properties named in the SETFROMREQUEST tag will be set to the values of the implicitly or explicitly specified request parameters in the tag.

The syntax for a SETFROMREQUEST tag can be one of the following three forms.

```
<SETFROMREQUEST
    BEANPROPERTY = "property name"
    PARAMNAME = "parameter name">
```

Sets the Bean property specified by the BEANPROPERTY attribute to the value of the request parameter specified by the PARAMNAME attribute.

```
<SETFROMREQUEST
    BEANPROPERTY = "property name">
```

A Bean property is matched to a request parameter with the same name, and the Bean property is assigned the value of the request parameter.

```
<SETFROMREQUEST
    BEANPROPERTY = "*">
```

All Bean properties are matched to request parameters by assigning the wildcard character "*" to the BEANPROPERTY attribute.

JSP Bean Property Display Tags

Bean property can be accessed and then displayed either by the <DISPLAY...> tag for single-valued properties or by a combination of the <DISPLAY...> tag and <LOOP...></LOOP> tag pair for multivalued (for example, array) properties.

A new naming convention is used to fully qualify Bean property names in the property display tags. Because a Bean property can be a Bean containing further properties, the naming convention has to be hierarchical. Similar to EBNF, the syntax for the hierarchical naming convention of a property name is:

```
[beanname:]+propertyname
```

An example for an instance of a Bank Account Bean named bankAccount containing a property named debit is:

```
bankAccount:debit
```

The syntax for a DISPLAY tag is:

```
<DISPLAY
    PROPERTY = "[beanname:]+propertyname"
    PLACEHOLDER = "fall back value">
```

The DISPLAY tag displays the value of a Bean property specified by the PROPERTY attribute. If the property's value is missing or invalid, then the value of the PLACEHOLDER value is displayed.

To display a multivalued Bean property, use a combination of LOOP and DISPLAY tags. The syntax for the simplest combination is:

```
<LOOP PROPERTY="[beanname:]+propertyname"
  PROPERTYELEMENT="x">
    <DISPLAY PROPERTY="x" PLACEHOLDER = "fall back value">
</LOOP>
```

The LOOP tag is used to iterate through all the elements of a multivalued attribute. The current element is identified by the name specified in the PROPERYELEMENT attribute. This name is subsequently used in the DISPLAY tag to display the value of the current element.

JSP Conditional Tags

Two tags—INCLUDEIF and EXCLUDEIF—provided by JavaServer Pages enable the conditional exclusion or inclusion of any code consisting of valid JSP syntax. The conditionality is based on a Bean property value matching a particular value specified inside the tags.

The syntax of the INCLUDEIF tag pair is:

```
<INCLUDEIF PROPERTY = "[beanname:]+propertyname"
    VALUE="value to match"
    CASE="sensitive|insesitive"
     MATCH="null|exact|contains|startswith|endswidth">
```

and

```
</INCLUDEIF>
```

The syntax of the EXCLUDEIF tag pair is:

```
<EXCLUDEIF PROPERTY = "[beanname:]+propertyname"
    VALUE="value to match"
    CASE="sensitive|insensitive"
     MATCH="null|exact|contains|startswith|endswidth">
```

and

```
</EXCLUDEIF>
```

The PROPERTY attribute specifies the Bean property that is being matched against the value specified by the VALUE attribute. The optional CASE attribute is used to specify whether the matching should be case sensitive (for appropriate Bean property types, such as String or char). If the Bean property is of type String, then the matching between the PROPERTY and VALUE attribute can be customized with the MATCH attribute. For the matching behavior for each of the possible values, the MATCH attribute that can be assigned is as follows.

- **null**. The VALUE attribute is ignored. The value of the Bean property is matched against null.

- **exact**. The value specified by the VALUE attribute must exactly match the string value of the Bean property. This is the default behavior of the conditional tags if the MATCH attribute is not supplied.

- **contains**. The string value specified by the VALUE attribute must appear as a substring within the string value of the Bean property.

- **startswith**. The string value specified by the VALUE attribute must appear as a substring at the beginning of the string value of the Bean property.

- **endswith**. The string value specified by the VALUE attribute must appear as a substring at the end of the string value of the Bean property.

Implicit Beans

JavaServer Pages provides two implicit Beans, named exception and request, that do not require a USEBEAN tag prior to their use in a page.

- **Exception Bean** — An error Bean that holds information on the most recent error in a .jsp page request in which the ERRORPAGE directive appears (see "JavaServer Pages Scripting-Centric Tags" on page 133). The exception Bean is an instance of the java.langThrowable class that provides methods for exception handling and diagnostics.

- **Request Bean** — Request parameters, request headers, and CGI-like environment variables of an incoming client request are made available through the request Bean. The request Bean properties are accessible from within the DISPLAY, INCLUDEIF, and EXCLUDEIF tags. Refer to the JavaServer Pages specification for the available methods.

JavaServer Pages Example

The following example illustrates the use of JavaServer Pages. The first part is the JSP page, the second is the JavaBean code invoked by the JSP page. In this example, when the page is invoked, a counter is incremented and displayed.

```
<html>
<usebean name="cbean" type = counter.Counter lifespan =
   application>
<setoncreate beanproperty=imageDirectory
   value="/images/counter/">
<setoncreate beanproperty=imageName value="ocr.gif">
</usebean>

This page has been accessed <DISPLAY property=cbean:counter>
   times.

</html>

package counter;
import java.io.*;
import java.util.*;
import javax.servlet.http.*;

public class Counter {

    int counter = 0;
    String imageDir = "/DOCROOT/images/counter/";
    String imagePrefix = "<img src=" + imageDir;
    String imageName = "number.gif";
    String imageSuffix = imageName + ">";

    public static void main(String args[]) {
Counter c = new Counter();
c.processRequest(null);
    }


    public void processRequest(HttpServletRequest req) {
counter++;
    }


    public void setImageDirectory(String image) {
```

```
imageDir = image;
imagePrefix = "<img src=" + imageDir;
    }

    public void setImageName(String n) {
imageName = n;
imageSuffix = imageName + ">";
    }


    public int getHits() {
return counter;
    }

    public String getCounter() {
StringBuffer s = new StringBuffer();
String count = new Integer(counter).toString();
char c[] = count.toCharArray();
for (int i = 0; i < c.length; i++) {
    String img = imagePrefix + c[i] + imageSuffix;
    s.append(img);
}
return s.toString();
    }
}
```

Chapter **10**

Putting the Theory to Work

To bring to life the theory we have discussed so far, we created a small scenario. The first section starts by introducing the scenario and the requirements that the new system must satisfy. Subsequent sections go through the process of developing and deploying the system.

Introducing the Situation

Henri has a very successful restaurant, called Henri's Stuffed Peppers. Like all successful business people, Henri wants to expand his business and become even more successful. His customers have been telling him about the Internet and how convenient it would be if they could place orders for his delicious stuffed peppers over the Internet. Seeing a potential market opportunity, Henri decides to investigate the Internet.

Henri contacts one of his customers, Rashik, who happens to work for IBM. After a long discussion and after listening to the problem facing Henri, Rashik suggests that a solution using IBM e-business technology would be the best solution. He suggests that Henri first provide an online ordering service for the customers. Henri agrees and asks Rashik to give him more information.

Rashik can provide all the infrastructure components Henri will need:

- A Web server — Lotus Domino Go

- An Enterprise JavaBeans server — IBM WebSphere Application Server

- A database — DB2

- A connection to the Internet

- A managed firewall service to stop competitors from tampering with his service

Since Rashik does not have access to developers who can build applications, he contacts a business partner with experience in building Internet-based systems— Dani's Rapid Application Assembly, Inc. Dani and Henri discuss the requirements, and Dani contracts to build the system.

Dani knows that there are a number of EJBs that he could use to speed up the development and, most importantly, to keep the cost down. Dani contacts Thea's Bean Factory Outlet to check what Beans are available. He finds that he can use some of the Beans and orders them.

Rashik returns to see Henri a few days later with Dani to provide a proposal. Henri has had experience with software projects before. When he ordered the accounting system, the vendor promised it would be implemented in one month. It took three months, and the vendor never delivered all the promised facilities. This time, Henri wants to make sure that his software is delivered on time and, most importantly, that the service will be reliable.

Unlike last time, this time Henri's customers are going to be using this system, which will become one of Henri's shop windows. So, Henri, being a shrewd businessman, negotiates an attractive price and favorable terms. After the meeting, he is feeling pleased that this time he has a team he can trust and who can deliver the solution he needs at a price he can afford.

Rashik makes it clear that Henri needs someone to manage the solution. Rashik says that it is important that the person who will manage the system be involved from the beginning; otherwise, there will always be problems. One of the local personal computer manufacturing plants has recently closed down, and one of Henri's customers, Doug, used to work there. Henri decides to ask Doug if he would be willing to work for Henri to install (deploy) and manage the solution that Rashik and Dani will build. Doug is delighted and accepts Henri's offer without hesitation.

A few weeks later, Dani has built the system by customizing Thea's EJBs, and Rashik and Dani provide a demonstration to Henri and Doug. Henri is delighted with the system and wants it installed the following week.

Henri's online ordering is a huge success. He has increased his lunchtime business ten times over. The customers are now asking Henri to deliver the peppers to their offices and homes.

Henri does not want to employ a driver or have the problems of managing a fleet of cars. After all, his speciality is stuffed peppers. However, the average delivery company will not suffice. He needs to find a delivery company that can handle the stuffed peppers with care. He needs a delivery company that is fast, reliable, and has an image that will complement the image he has now developed.

Then he remembers his friend, Jürgen, who has a delivery service. Henri wonders what kind of service Jürgen provides and decides to contact him. Jürgen, being a stylish German, has created an exclusive delivery service, Jürgen's Ultimate Miata Powered Delivery Service (Jump DS). As the name suggests, Jürgen's fleet consists of only Miatas.

Henri visits Jürgen and is impressed with the business he has built. They discuss Henri's requirements, and they agree that Jürgen will provide delivery for Henri's stuffed peppers.

Henri is then faced with another set of problems: How does he notify Jürgen that the peppers are ready for delivery and where they should be delivered? Then he has an idea. He could extend his ordering service to provide delivery information to Jürgen.

He contacts Doug to check if that makes sense, and Doug says that will be possible if Dani writes some more EJBs. Dani provides Doug with the extensions, using more EJBs from Thea's Bean Factory Outlet. Doug sets up Jürgen's systems to allow the EJBs to be deployed.

Figure 10–1 illustrates the scenario; now let's build the applications to support the scenario. Let's start by analyzing the problem and creating an object model.

Analyzing the Problem Domain

Describing the Problem

Henri wants to enter a new market by offering his Stuffed Peppers menus through an online ordering system on the Internet. Online ordering will allow customers to connect through the Internet to the ordering system. The customer will be able to select from a list of items. The customer's selection will then get transferred to the server. The server will calculate a price for the items and send

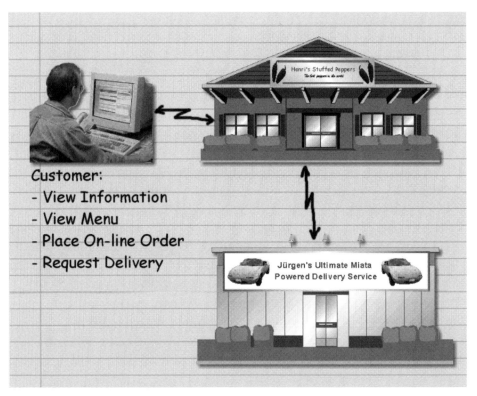

Customer:
- View Information
- View Menu
- Place On-line Order
- Request Delivery

Figure 10–1   *Overall Scenario*

the price back to the client. The customer can either accept or decline. If the customer accepts, an order will be printed at the restaurant.

Modeling the Requirements, Using Use Cases

Use Case modeling is one of the most common means of analyzing business requirements. The requirements are viewed from a user's perspective rather than from concern about the internal structure of a system that will be built. Use Cases describe individual business processes or scenarios for an abstract system.

A Use Case is normally triggered by an actor substituting either a human user or another system interacting with the system to be described. In the Use Case model, the actors are represented by little figures connected to the relevant Use Cases.

The Use Case model shown in Figure 10–2 illustrates the relevant business functions that Henri's online ordering system must provide. This functionality is incomplete when compared to a real-world solution, but it provides enough functionality for our samples.

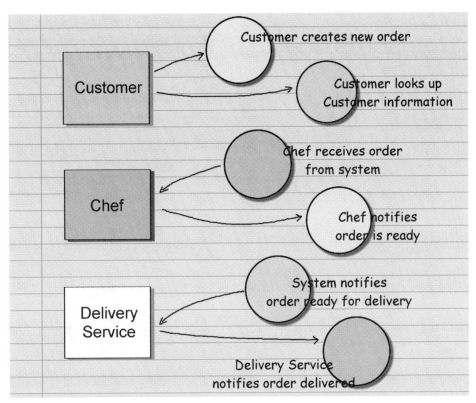

Figure 10–2 *Use Case Model*

In a real project, one would describe each Use Case in greater detail than is shown in Figure 10–2, addressing the following areas:

- Detailed description of the business scenario

- Prerequisites to run the scenario

- Result(s)

- User actions necessary to run the scenario

- Assumptions and exceptions

However, for our little sample project, the Use Case model provides enough insight into the business functionality to enable us to proceed.

Now that we understand the system requirements, we must analyze the entities and their associations.

The Object Model Analysis

The Object Model is described in Figure 10–3. The main entities are `Customer`, `Order`, `Product`, and `Payment`. `Henri's Restaurant` will use n instances of `Customer`. The `Customer` places 0 to n `Orders` requiring one `Payment`. Each `Order` selects a `Product`.

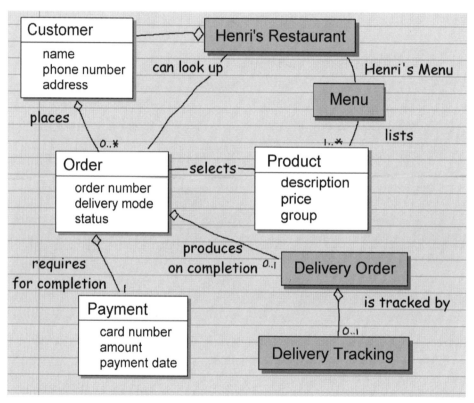

Figure 10–3 *Analysis Object Model*

Designing the System

Once we have completed the object analysis, we are ready to start designing the system.

The following model illustrates our design of Henri's online ordering system. To keep the design as simple as possible, while still allowing us to demonstrate the various flavors of Enterprise Java Beans, we made some simplifications one would normally not do in a real model.

For example, we omitted the classes representing the `Henri's Restaurant` entity (which would hold information about the restaurant such as the address, telephone number, etc.) as well as the `Menu` entity.

Furthermore, we added the payment-related information to the `Order` class to eliminate the `Payment` business entity one would probably implement in a more mature system.

We introduced three new classes representing the behavior of the system with regards to the different users. These classes implement the business rules and are often referred to as Application objects.

The Design Object Model

Our design plan leaves us with the Design Object Model (DOM) shown in Figure 10–4.

The purpose of the entity classes `Customer`, `Order`, `Product`, `ProdOrd`, and `DeliveryOrder` is pretty much self-explanatory. Instances of these classes need to be kept persistent and will therefore be represented by Entity Beans.

The `CustomerSession` implements the system behavior relevant to a customer connected through the Internet. It lets a customer sign in for the first time by creating a new `customer` entity object to be filled with all the relevant information about the new customer.

The `ChefSession` represents the system functionality for letting the chef notify the system that an order has been completed and is ready for delivery or pickup.

The `DeliverySession` represents the functionality provided to the delivery service. It lets the delivery service update the status of the `DeliveryOrder` after the order has been delivered to the customer (or, maybe, nondelivery because the customer provided the wrong address).

Some Object Interaction Diagrams

To understand the dynamic aspects of our online ordering system, we provide some Object Interaction Diagrams (OIDs) that illustrate the flow of messages between the classes (that is, the calling order of the methods).

The first OID, shown in Figure 10–5, illustrates the creation of a new order under two different circumstances:

1. A new customer applies and places an order.

2. An existing customer places an order.

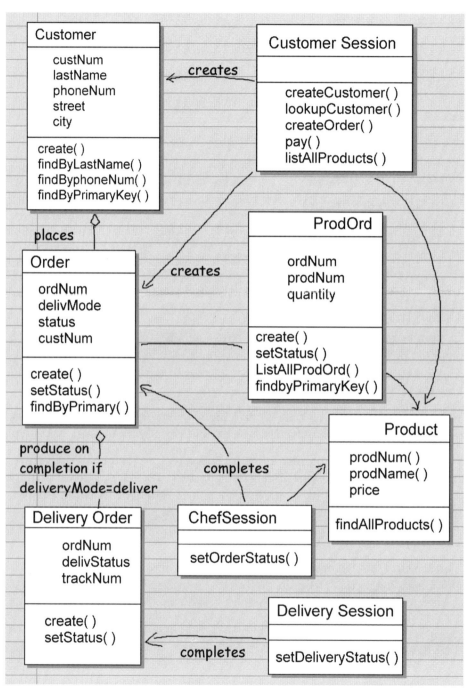

Figure 10–4 *Design Object Model*

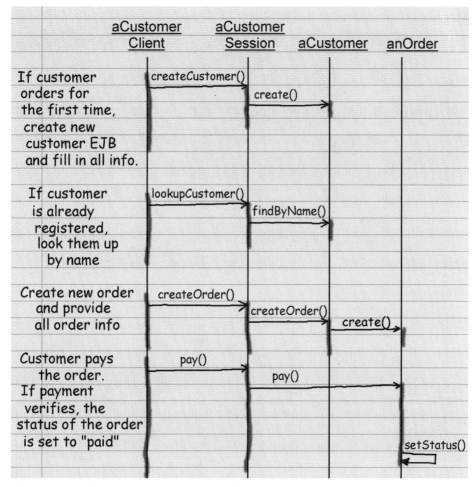

Figure 10–5 *OID: Create New Order*

After the `Order` is created and passed to `theChef`, which notifies the system when the order is ready, a delivery order is generated. Figure 10–6 illustrates the process.

Then, the delivery service takes over and delivers the order, marking the end of the full cycle. Figure 10–7 illustrates the process.

This model design is simplified. In real life, things like payment validation and updating the customer entries have to be considered.

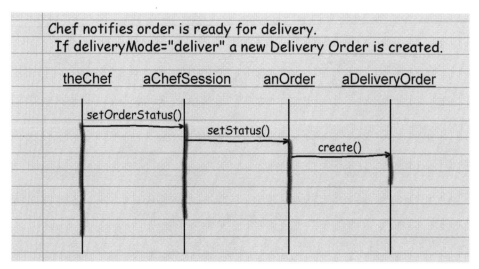

Figure 10–6   *OID: Chef Notifies Order Is Ready*

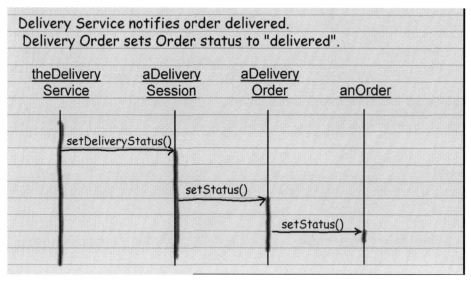

Figure 10–7   *OID: Delivery Service Notifies Order Is Delivered*

Phasing the Development

We now have a system design that will form the basis of the development work. However, we have to learn a little more about EJBs before we start to write the whole system. So, we start by writing our first EJB. Like most developers, we will develop the system in stages.

1. **SimpleCustomer.** Developing a simple Session Bean and client will help us gain a practical understanding of the development environment and also the runtime infrastructure.

2. **An Entity Bean and a Session Bean.** In this sample, we will develop the Product Entity Bean and a customer session. To test these, we will develop a JavaServer Page that uses a Java Bean to access the customer session and the product Entity EJBs.

3. **The Internet-based ordering system.** We will build on the second sample and add the order and customer entity EJBs. These will show both Bean-managed and Entity-managed persistence.

For all these examples, we have used the IBM Enterprise JavaBean tools. These are described in more detail in "Products" on page 193.

The remainder of the section explains the development and deployment of each of these samples. For each sample, we explain the objectives, how they relate to the overall scenario, the solution, and any conclusions we can draw from the project.

Sample 1 — Creating a SimpleCustomer Session Bean

Here, we introduce a simple example to illustrate and provide a practical understanding of some of the EJB concepts introduced in the earlier chapters. We also introduce the EJB development environment of VisualAge for Java and describe how to develop, test, and run EJBs within that environment.

Relationship to the Overall Scenario

This sample introduces a session EJB. We use variation of this EJB with more methods and business logic, although we don't use this variation in the later samples.

This sample illustrates the following steps.

1. How to write a simple stateful session EJB

2. How to access an EJB from a simple client

The basic scenario is that we want to record the details of a customer (for example, customer's name, address, and so on) into the fields of an EJB. The details will not be stored for posterity because we will use a stateful Session Bean that does not have any persistence framework.

Entity Beans that do provide a persistence framework will be used in samples 2 and 3. For brevity, and so as not to distract from the main purpose of this example, the only detail that will be recorded is the customer's name.

SimpleCustomer Architecture

The EJB components of sample 1 are illustrated in Figure 10–8 and described below. For a more detailed explanation about Session Beans, containers, and EJB servers, see "EJB Architecture Elements" on page 19.

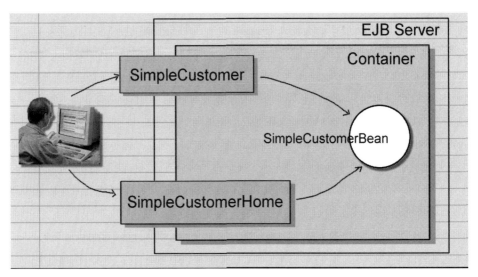

Figure 10–8 *Sample 1 Architecture*

Enterprise JavaBean (EJB) (`SimpleCustomer`)

`SimpleCustomer` is a stateful Session EJB. Unlike stateless Session Beans, which are pooled by a container per method invocation, stateful Session Beans exist for the entire duration of a single client/server session.

For its state information, `SimpleCustomer` contains one field called `custName`, which is of type String. Two methods are also defined and implemented: an accessor and modifier method for the `custName` field (`getCustName()` and `setCustName()`, respectively).

Home Interface (`SimpleCustomerHome`)

In this sample, VAJ generates a `create()` method in the `SimpleCustomer` home interface. The `create()` method enables a client to generate a `SimpleCustomer` EJB. A client locates a home interface through the standard Java Naming and Directory Interface (JNDI).

Remote Interface (`SimpleCustomer`)

The remote interface `SimpleCustomer`, specifies the business methods made available to a client. The method names and signatures declared in the remote interface exactly match those defined and implemented in the EJB. In this sample, the accessor and modifier methods will be promoted to the remote interface and hence made visible.

Prerequisites for Our Sample1

Before you can begin the sample, you must have VisualAge for Java installed and configured.

Creating the EJBatWork Project in VisualAge for Java

Projects are units of organization that group Java packages in VisualAge for Java. All of the samples illustrated in this book are grouped in the same project. The following steps illustrate how to create an `EJBatWork` project in VisualAge for Java that will be used by all the samples.

1. If the All Projects pane isn't currently selected in the Workbench window, click on the **Projects** tab (see Figure 10–9).

2. In the All Projects pane, click the right mouse button and select **Add -> Project** (see Figure 10–10). The Add Project Smart Guide opens.

3. In the Create a new project named: field, type `EJBatWork`.

4. Click **Finish** to create the project. The project is displayed in the All Projects pane.

Creating the SimpleCustomer EJB

The EJB Development Environment of VisualAge for Java (VAJ) allows a programmer to develop, test, and then run EJBs, all within VAJ. We use VAJ to write a SimpleCustomer EJB in this section. In the next section, we develop a simple

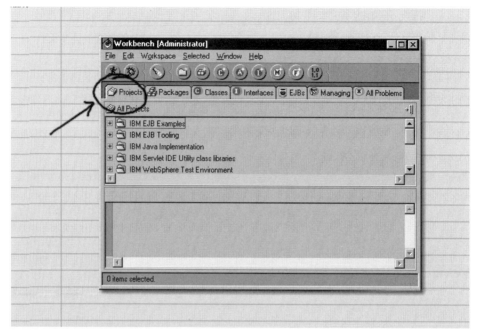

Figure 10–9 *Workbench: Project Pane*

command-line client application to test the SimpleCustomer EJB developed in this section.

The lists in this section lead you through the process of developing the Simple-Customer EJB within VisualAge for Java.

- If the All Projects pane is not currently selected in the Workbench window, click on the **Projects** tab.

- Click the right mouse button on **EJBatWork**, then select **Add -> Package**; the Add Package Smart Guide opens.

- In the Create a new package named: field, type `com.ibm.ejbatwork.beans` and click **Finish**.

- Click on the **EJBs** tab in the **Workbench** window (see Figure 10–11). The EJBs pane appears.

Although EJBs become part of a project within VAJ, they also have their own dedicated grouping structure, called an EJB group. An EJB group provides the necessary support for maintaining EJB code. For this sample, we create a group called

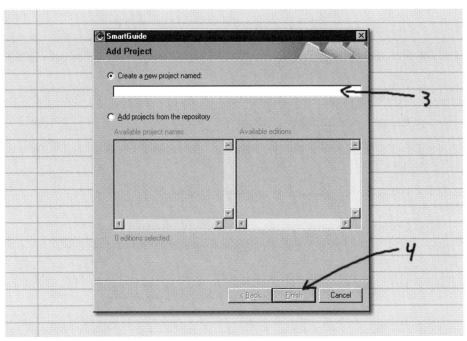

Figure 10–10 *Workbench: Add Projects*

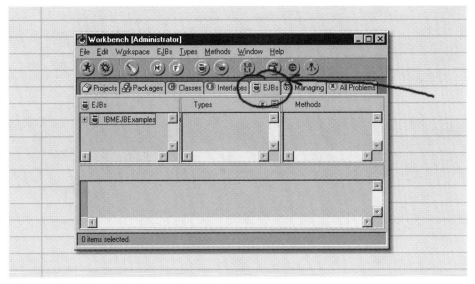

Figure 10–11 *Workbench: EJBs Pane*

`EJBatWorkSamp1`, which will contain the `SimpleCustomer` Session Bean and related code. Continuing our process:

- Click with the right mouse button in the EJBs column of the EJBs pane. Select **Add -> EBJ Group**; the **Add EJB Group** Smart Guide opens.

- In the **Project** field, type `EJBatWork`.

- In the Create a new EJB named: field, type `EJBatWorkSamp1`.

- Click **Finish**. The group EJBatWorkSamp1 is created and displayed in the EJBs pane.

We can now create the EJB. Continuing our process:

- Select **EJBatWorkSamp1**, then click with right mouse button and select **Add -> EJB**. The Create EJB Smart Guide appears (see Figure 10–12).

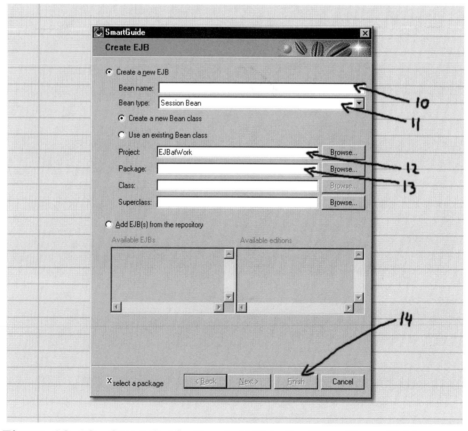

Figure 10–12 *Smart Guide: Create EJB in the Bean Name Field*

- In the Project field (arrow 12, in the figure), ensure that `EJBatWork` is displayed.

- In the Package field (arrow 13, in the figure), ensure that `com.ibm.ejbatwork.beans` is displayed.

- In the Class field, ensure that `SimpleCustomerBean` is displayed.

- Click **Finish** (arrow 14, in the figure). The `SimpleCustomer` EJB appears under the group `EJBatWork` in the EJBs column.

We can now add the `custName` String field, and the corresponding accessor and modifier methods for this field. Continuing our process:

- In the Types column of the EJBs pane, select the **simpleCustomerBean** class, then click with right mouse button and select **Add -> Field**. The Create Field Smart Guide appears (see Figure 10–13).

- In the Field Name: field (arrow 16, in Figure 10–13), type `custName`.

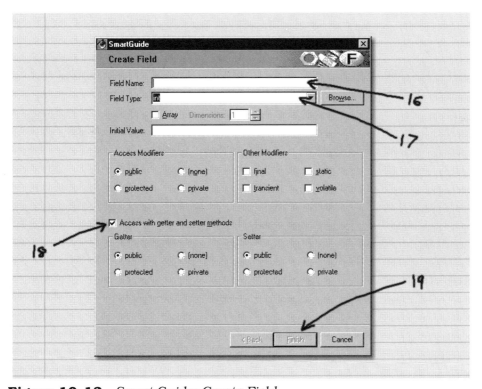

Figure 10-13 *Smart Guide: Create Field*

- In the Field Type: field (arrow 17, in the figure), select **java.lang.String** from the drop-down box.

- Ensure that the **Access with getter and setter methods** check box is selected (arrow 18, in the figure).

- Click the **Finish** button (arrow 19). In the Methods column of the EJBs pane, two methods will appear: `getCustNum()` and `setCustNum()`. For this sample, we need not modify the body of the two methods because the default VAJ-generated implementations of the methods will suffice.

Now, to make the `getCustNum()` and `setCustNum()` methods visible to client, we need to promote the methods to the `SimpleCustomer` Remote Interface. Continuing our process:

- Click the right mouse button on the **getCustNum()** method, then select **Add to -> EJB Remote Interface**. Repeat for the `setCustNum()` method.

  Note: If you click on the **SimpleCustomer Interface** in the types column, you will not find the two methods declared there yet. First the deployed code needs to be generated, as described in the last bulleted item.

- In the EJBs column of the EJBs pane, click the right mouse button on the **simpleCustomer EJB** and select **Properties**. For the `SimpleCustomer` EJB, the dialog box shown in Figure 10–14 is displayed.

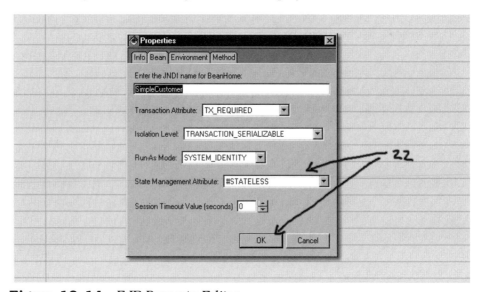

Figure 10–14 *EJB Property Editor*

- In the State Management Attribute field, select **#STATEFUL** from the drop-down box and press **OK** (as shown by arrow 22 in Figure 10–14).

- Click the right mouse button on the **SimpleCustomer EJB** and select **Generate -> Deployed Code.**

This last step generates the EJBObject and Home implementations and implementation classes for the home and remote interface. Stubs and skeletons that are required for RMI access over IIOP are also generated, as are helper classes and holders for the home and remote interfaces.

The `SimpleCustomer` Bean is now ready to be run and tested, as described in the following sections.

A Simple Client for the SimpleCustomer EJB

Now, we develop a simple command-line client to perform the following tasks.

- Locate the `SimpleCustomer`'s home interface, using JNDI

- Create an instance of the `SimpleCustomer` Session Bean

- Call methods within the `SimpleCustomer`'s remote interface

See "JNDI Example" on page 118, which describes and shows Java code snippets used to locate a EJB's home interface by means of JNDI.

The following steps develop a simple command-line client for the `SimpleCustomer` EJB.

1. If the All Projects pane isn't currently selected in the Workbench window, click on the **Projects** tab.

2. Click the right mouse button on **EJBatWork**, then select **Add -> Package**. The Add Package Smart Guide opens.

3. In the Create a new package named: field, type `com.ibm.ejbatwork.clients` and click **Finish**.

4. Click the right mouse button on **com.ibm.ejbatwork.clients** package in the All Projects pane, then select **Add -> Class**. The Create Class Smart Guide appears.

5. In the Class Name: field, type `SimpleCustomerClient`.

6. Click on the **Next** button; the Create Class Smart Guide changes to an Attributes Smart Guide.

7. Select the **main(String[])** check box.

8. Click on the **Add Package** button; an Import statement dialog box appears.

9. In the Pattern field, type com.ibm.ejbatwork; **com.ibm.ejbatwork.clients** appears in the Names scrolling list. Select it by clicking on it. Click on the **Finish** button.

10. Click on the **Finish** button in the Attributes Smart Guide.

11. Expand the SimpleCustomer Class entry in the All Projects pane and select the **main[String[])** method.

12. Modify the implementation of the main() method in the Source pane to be the following.

```java
/**
 * Starts the SimpleCustomerClt application.
 * @param args an array of command-line arguments
 */
public static void main(java.lang.String[] args) {
    SimpleCustomerHome simpleCustomerHome = null;
    javax.naming.InitialContext initContext = null;
    com.ibm.jndi.CosNaming.CNInitialContextFactory factory = null;

    // Get the initial context
    try {
      System.out.println("Retrieving initial context...");
      java.util.Hashtable properties = new java.util.Hashtable(2);
      // name server on localhost
      properties.put(javax.naming.Context.PROVIDER_URL, "iiop:///");
      // IBM name services
      properties.put(javax.naming.Context.INITIAL_CONTEXT_FACTORY,
              "com.ibm.jndi.CosNaming.CNInitialContextFactory");
      initContext = new javax.naming.InitialContext(properties);
    }catch (javax.naming.NamingException e) {
      System.out.println("Error retrieving the initial context: " +
          e.getMessage());
      System.exit(0);
    } // end try

    // look up the home interface, using the JNDI name
    try {
      System.out.println("Retrieving the home interface...");
      // "SimpleCustomer" is the JNDI name of the home interface
      java.lang.Object o = initContext.lookup("SimpleCustomer");
      if (o instanceof org.omg.CORBA.Object)
        simpleCustomerHome =
          SimpleCustomerHomeHelper.narrow((org.omg.CORBA.Object) o);
      } catch (javax.naming.NamingException e) {
```

```
          System.out.println("Error retrieving the home interface: "
            + e.getMessage());
        System.exit(0);
      // end try

      // Create a new SimpleCustomer
      System.out.println("Creating new SimpleCustomer...");
      SimpleCustomer simpleCustomer = null;
      try {
        simpleCustomer = simpleCustomerHome.create();
        System.out.println("SimpleCustomer created!");
      catch (Exception e) {
        System.out.println("Exception creating new SimpleCustomer: "
          + e.getMessage());
        System.exit(0);
      // end try

      // call the setter and getter methods for the custName property
      try {
        System.out.println();
        System.out.println("Setting the custName property to \"Henri\"");
        simpleCustomer.setCustName("Henri");
        System.out.println("Getting the customerName:");
        System.out.print("\tcustName = \"");
        System.out.println(simpleCustomer.getCustName() + "\"");
      catch (Exception e) {
        System.out.println("Exception iterating through Enumerations: " + e);
        System.exit(0);
      // end try
}
```

13. The final step of creating the SimpleCustomer client is to configure the client's CLASSPATH so that the client can find the necessary classes at runtime. With the right mouse button, click on the **SimpleCustomer** Class entry in the All Project pane and select **Properties**. A Properties for SimpleCustomerClt dialog box appears.

14. Click the **Class Path** tab.

15. Click on the **Compute Now** button. This action will automatically determine the classpath required by the client. In the **Project Path** field, IBM WebSphere Test Environment appears.

16. At the bottom of the Properties dialog, select the **Save in repository (as default)** check box and click **OK**.

Before we can run the client, we first need to start a server (see the next section) for the SimpleCustomer EJB.

EJB Server for SimpleCustomer EJB

After the `SimpleCustomer` EJB has been written and the deployed classes generated (see "Creating the SimpleCustomer EJB" on page 153), we can create an EJB server configuration in which the `SimpleCustomer` EJB can be run. Before the EJB server is started, the JNDI name server must be started (in VisualAge for Java, the JNDI name server consists of two servers: the Location Service daemon and Persistent Name server).

Running the EJB server for the `EJBatWorkSamp1` Group, which contains the `SimpleCustomer` Session Bean, is done as follows.

- Click on the **EJBs** tab in the in the Workbench window.
- With the right mouse button click on the **EJBatWorkSamp1** Group and then select **Add to -> Server Configuration**. The EJB Server Configuration browser appears.
- In the Servers pane, click with right mouse button on the **Location Service Daemon** and then select **Start Server**. A Console window appears.
- In the Servers pane, click with right mouse button on the **Persistent Name Server** and then select **Start Server**.
- In the Console that appears, check that the **Location Service Daemon** and **Persistent Name Server** are running by selecting each one (arrow 5, in Figure 10–15). Something like the following messages appear.
  ```
  Location service daemon listening ...
  NameServer is listening ...
  ```
- In the Servers pane, click with right mouse button on the **EJB Server (server 1)** (arrow 7, in the figure) and then select **Start Server**.

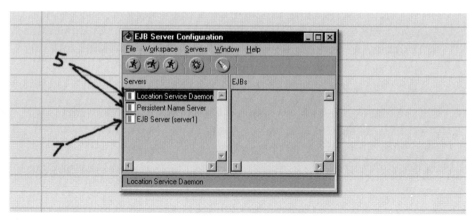

Figure 10–15 *EJB Server Configuration Console*

- In the Console, click on the last entry in the **All Programs** list to see the output of the EJB Server for the `SimpleCustomer` Session Bean. The third-to-last line of the console output should contain the following line indicating that the server is ready.

```
Server is listening...
```

Running the Simple Client for the SimpleCustomer EJB

We can now test `SimpleCustomer` EJB we developed by the simple command-line client that was written in "A Simple Client for the SimpleCustomer EJB" on page 159.

1. Click with right mouse button on **SimpleCustomerClt** Class in the All Projects Pane and select **Run -> Run main**.

2. Click on **com.ibm.ejbatwork.clients.SimpleCustomerClt** in the Console window to see the output of the client. The following messages will appear in the standard output window of the Console:

```
Retrieving initial context...
Retrieving the home interface...
Creating new SimpleCustomer...
SimpleCustomer created!

Setting the custName property to "Henri"
Getting the custName:
custName = "Henri"
```

Conclusion

In completing this sample, you have now implemented the development environment for EJB, developed an EJB, implemented the runtime EJB infrastructure, created a container for the EJB, and executed the EJB by using a Java Client application.

We are now ready to develop Henri's online order entry application.

Sample 2 — Creating the Product and Customer Session EJBs

In this section, we illustrate the development and deployment of a container-managed Entity Bean—`Product`. At the same time, this sample introduces JavaServer Pages for client-side processing.

Relationship to the Scenario

This sample will allow a customer to view the product menu that is provided by Henri's Stuffed Peppers restaurant. It implements the CustomerSession and Products portion of the object model. In addition, to allow access to these EJBs from a browser, a JSP and associated customer client Java Bean will be developed.

Sample 2 Structure — How It Works

Figure 10–16 shows the overall structure for the sample that we will be developing and deploying.

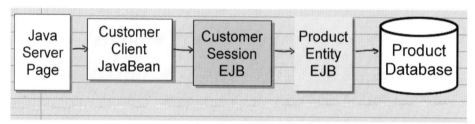

Figure 10–16 *Sample 2 Overall Structure*

Before we develop the sample, let us run through how the sample will work when implemented.

- A JSP page request is made by a browser.

- The JSP page is dynamically compiled into a servlet (if accessing the JSP page for the first time).

- The servlet creates an instance of a `MenuDataBean` Java Bean.

- The `MenuDataBean` Bean creates a new `CustomerSession` EJB.

- `CustomerSession` invokes `findAllProducts()` method of `Product`.

- `Product` initiates an SQL statement to retrieve all the products stored on the database and creates product entities for all the products. It then returns an `Enumeration` of `Product`.

- `CustomerSession` returns the product `Enumeration` to `MenuDataBean`.

- `MenuDataBean` iterates through the `Product Enumeration` and stores the product name, product number, and price fields of each Product Entity EJB as elements of three corresponding, multivalued properties of the `MenuDataBean`.

- The JSP (or, more correctly, JSP-generated servlet) uses the `MenuDataBean`'s get methods to retrieve the product name, product number, and price for all the products that have been retrieved. These data are inserted into the appropriate places in the JSP.

- The resulting HTML is sent to the browser. A product menu appears on the browser.

This is how it will all work once we have developed the Beans, so here goes. But, you have a decision to make first. There are two possible paths from here. The first, detailed below, is to create the samples from scratch. The second path is based on the "chef on the television show" approach of using the sample we prepared earlier. This approach is detailed in "Loading the Sample Code from the CD-ROM" on page 174. Both these paths will come together to run the sample within VAJ and then will be deployed in WebSphere.

Overview of the Code for This Sample

Before we start to code the samples, let's walk through the code. We will start with the `ProductEntity` Bean, move on to the `CustomerSession` Bean, the `MenuDataBean` JavaBean, and the JSP.

Product Entity EJB

The `Product` container-managed Entity Bean consists of two classes and three interfaces.

The two classes are:

- `ProductKey`
  This class defines the key field that is the integer `ProdNum` in this sample. We will also provide three productKey() signatures. The first signature has no parameters and returns a product numbered 0. The second uses an integer. The third signature uses a Product Bean.

- `ProductBean`
  This class implements the business function for the Bean. For this sample we do not need to write any specific business functions, so we use those that VisualAge creates by default: `ejbActivate()`, `ejbCreate()`, `ejbLoad()`, `ejbPassivate()`, `ejbPostCreate()`, `ejbRemove()`, `ejbStore()`, `setEntityContext()`, and `unsetEntityContext()`. In addition, we will require three methods to access the `prodNum`, `prodName`, and `price` fields.

The three interfaces are:

- `Product`
  This interface defines the remote interface for the EJB itself. For our sample, there are three accessor methods for retrieving the product information: `getProdNum()`, `getProdName()`, and `getPrice()`.

- `ProductHome`
  This interface defines the home interface for the Product EJB. For our sample, we are only interested in the `findAllProducts()` method. However, VisualAge automatically defines a `create()` and a `findByPrimaryKey()` method.

- `ProductBeanHelperFinder`
  In the sample, we want to be able to find all the products that are held in the database. Because we have to provide an SQL statement to find all the products in the database, we use the statement `select * from EJB.ProductBeanTbl`.

CustomerSession EJB

For the `CustomerSession` Bean, we will create a simple session Bean that has one additional remote interface: `listAllProducts`. When we create the Bean, VisualAge will create two interfaces:

- `CustomerSession`
  This interface implements the remote interface to the EJB. The only remote interface we will implement is `listAllProducts()`.

- `CustomerSessionHome`
  This interface implements the home interface. Here, we will only have the default `create()` interface created by VisualAge.

VisualAge also creates a default `CustomerSessionBean` class with the default methods `ejbActivate()`, `ejbCreate()`, `ejbPassivate()`, `ejbPostCreate()`, `ejbRemove()`, `setSessionContext()`. We modify the `ejbCreate()` method to find the home interface for the Product Entity Bean, which we store in a private class field. Finally, we add a `listAllProducts` method that simply invokes the `findAllProducts()` method of the `ProductHome`, which is returned to the caller.

MenuDataBean Java Bean

This Bean is used by the JavaServer Page to retrieve the product details. An `initialize()` method is defined to find the home interface for the

`CustomerSession` and invoke its `listAllProducts` interface. The enumeration of products that are returned is then stored in an array. Three `get()` methods are defined for this class: `getProdNum()`, `getProdName()`, and `getPrice()`. These methods all use the Product EJBs get methods to return the appropriate field.

JavaServer Page

The last piece of the jigsaw puzzle is the Java Server Page to display the results. The three tags that do all the magic are:

```
<bean name="customerClient" type="com.ibm.ejbatwork.client.CustomerClient"
scope=session>
</bean>
```

```
<repeat>
<insert bean=customerClient property=prodName></insert>
</repeat>
```

The `<bean>` tag defines the Bean that we want to use—the `CustomerClient`. The `<repeat>` tag, as the name suggests, repeats the statements up to the `</repeat>`. The `<insert ...>` tag adds the value of a property of the Bean. Since the `<insert>` is within the `<repeat>` tag, the indexed value of the property is returned with the index starting at 0 through to the number of properties that have been defined.

You should now have a better understanding of the pieces that we will be building in the remainder of this section.

Creating the Code from Scratch

Here, we describe three Beans: `Product` Entity Bean, `CustomerSession` Bean, and `CustomerClient` Bean.

Create the Product Entity Bean

These are the steps necessary to create the `Product` Bean from scratch. Please refer to "Creating the SimpleCustomer EJB" on page 153 for a detailed description of the individual steps. The parameters in brackets are the names used in the examples on the CD-ROM.

1. Create a new project (`EJBatWork`).
2. Create a package within the new project (`com.ibm.ejbatwork.beans`).
3. Create an EJB Group (`EJBatWork`).
4. Create a new Entity EJB (`Product`).
    a. Select the EJB Group just created (`EJBatWork`).

    b. Press the right mouse button and select **Add -> Enterprise JavaBean**.

    c. Enter the Bean name (`Product`).

    d. Select the Bean type in the Entity Bean with container-managed persistence fields (**CMP**).

    e. Select the Project, using the Browse button (`EJBatWork`).

    f. Select the Package, using the Browse button (`com.ibm.ejbatwork.beans`).

    g. Click the **Finish** button.

This sequence of steps creates the following classes:

`Product`	The Bean's remote interface
`ProductBean`	The Bean's implementation class
`ProductBeanFinderHelper`	Helper class for the `finder()` methods
`ProductHome`	The home interface
`ProductKey`	Primary key class

5. Add the data fields to the `ProductBean` class. Note: Include the semicolons as shown in the data field names

    a. Replace
```
    public String primaryKey;
```
with
```
    public int prodNum;
```

    b. Add `public String prodName;`

    c. Add `public double price;`

    d. Edit the method `ejbCreate(ProductKey)` from:
```
    primaryKey = key.primaryKey;
```
to:
```
    prodNum = key.prodNum;
```

    Note: When saving this last modification, you will get an error message stating that the field named `prodNum` for the type named ...`ProductKey` is not defined.
Click on **Save**; the error will be resolved when we adapt the `ProductKey` class.

6. Add get methods for the `prodNum`, `prodName` and `price` fields to the `ProductBean` class and propagate the methods to the Bean's remote interface. (Note that we don't provide set methods because we don't want to allow an application to modify the product data in the database.)

a. In the Methods pane, select **Method Template** from the background menu (to add a new method to the `ProductBean` named `newMethod()`).

   b. Rename the method to `public int getProdNumber()` and add the statement:

```
return prodNum;
```

   c. Repeat the steps *a* and *b* for the `prodName` and `price` fields:

```
public String getProdName() { return prodName; }
public double getPrice() { return price }
```

   d. Add the above methods to the Beans remote interface by selecting **Add To -> EJB Remote Interface** in the right mouse-button menu on each of the three methods `getProdNumber()`, `getProdName()`, and `getPrice()`.

7.   Adapt the `ProductKey` class default implementation.

VisualAge for Java generated a default primary key class, `ProductKey`, for us. However, we must adapt the following parts of the class to match the model.

   a. Adapt the name and data type of the `primaryKey` instance variable from

```
public java.lang.String primaryKey;
```
to
```
public int prodNum;
```

   b. Adapt the `ProductKey()` constructor to

```
public ProductKey() {
prodNum = 0;
}
```

   c. Adapt the `ProductKey(String)` constructor to

```
public ProductKey(int aProdNum) {
this.prodNum = aProdNum;
}
```

This code actually adds a new constructor and leaves the old one untouched. Delete the `ProductKey(String)` constructor by selecting **Delete...** in the right mouse button menu on this method.

   d. Adapt the statement in `equals(Object)` from

```
return ((primaryKey.equals(otherKey.primaryKey)));
```
to
```
return (prodNum == otherKey.prodNum);
```

e. Adapt the statement in `hashCode()` from

```
return (primaryKey.hashCode());
```

to

```
return prodNum;
```

f. Add a new constructor method:

```
public ProductKey(ProductBean aProductBean) {
this.prodNum = aProductBean.prodNum;
}
```

After you complete the above steps, all the errors should be resolved (you should see no more red crosses in the Types or Method panes).

8. Add the `findAllProducts()` method to the `ProductHome` interface class so you can list all products. Note that this method returns an `Enumeration` of `Product` Bean remote objects.

- Add the following method to the `ProductHome` class:

```
public java.util.Enumeration findAllProducts()
    throws java.rmi.RemoteException, javax.ejb.FinderException;
```

9. Provide the SQL statement for the `findAllProducts()` finder method in the `ProductBeanFinderHelper` interface class. (**Note**: We don't need to provide the SQL statement for the `findByPrimaryKey()` finder method because it is automatically generated at deployment time.)

- Add the following new field to the `ProductBeanFinderHelper` class:

```
public static final String findAllProductsQueryString =
    "select * from ProductBeanTbl";
```

10. Set the properties of the `Product` Bean as follows (select the right mouse button menu **Properties** on the Bean):

a. **Transaction Attribute**: TX_SUPPORTS

b. **Isolation Level**: TRANSACTION_READ_COMMITTED

c. **Run-As Mode**: SYSTEM_IDENTITY

d. Check the **Reentrant** check box.

Create the CustomerSession Session Bean

1. Create a new Session EJB (`CustomerSession`).

a. Select the EJB Group just created (`EJBatWork`).

b. Press the right mouse button and select **Add -> Enterprise JavaBean**.

c. Enter the Bean name (`CustomerSession`).

d. Make sure the Bean type reads **SessionBean**.

    e. Select the project, using the Browse button (EJBatWork).

    f. Select the package, using the Browse button.
(com.ibm.ejbatwork.beans).

    g. Click the **Finish** button.

2. Add the listAllProducts() method to the bean.

    a. Select the **CustomerSessionBean** in the Types pane.

    b. Click the right mouse button and select **Add -> Method**.

    c. This method will be an Enumeration. So, click on the Types button and key in enu. **Enumeration** is displayed. Select it and click on the **Insert** button.

    d. Delete the text void newMethod and key in listAllProducts.

    e. Click on **Finish**.

    f. Edit the body of the method to be:

```
throws java.rmi.RemoteException
{    java.util.Enumeration products = null;
     try {products = productHome.findAllProducts();}
     catch(Exception e) {
          System.out.println("Error looking up Product EJBs:" + e);
          products = new java.util.Vector().elements();
     }
     return products;}
```

    g. Click on the **listAllProducts()** method in the Methods pane.

    h. Click the right mouse button and select **Add to -> Remote Interface**.

3. Modify the create() method to be the following:

```
public void ejbCreate() throws java.rmi.RemoteException {
  try {
       java.lang.Object obj = Utils.lookupFromURL(productJNDIName);
       productHome = ProductHomeHelper.narrow((org.omg.CORBA.Object)obj);
  } catch (javax.naming.NamingException e) {
       System.out.println("Error looking up Products: " + e);
       e.printStackTrace();
       throw new RemoteException(e.toString());
  }
}
```

Add the Utils Class

To simplify the code to find an EJBs home interface, we need to create a Utils class that implements one method: lookupFromURL().

1. Return to the **All Projects** tab.

2. Select the **com.ibm.ejbatwork.beans** package.

3. Click the right mouse button and select **Add Class**. Enter `Utils` for the class name. Ensure that the **Compose the Class Visually** is unchecked. Click on **Next**.

4. Uncheck the **Copy Constructors** from the superclass check box. Click on the **Add Package** button and select the **Java.util** package. Then, click on Finish.

5. In the Methods pane, click the right mouse button and select **Add Method**.

6. Type `Object lookupFromURL(String aURL)` for the method name. Click on **Next**. Ensure that **Public** and **Static** have been selected. Then, click on **Finish**.

7. Replace the body of this method with:

```
public static Object lookupFromURL(String aURL)
    throws javax.naming.NamingException
{ javax.naming.InitialContext context = null;
  Object result = null;
  final String iiopURLcontext - "iiop://";
  String lookupName = aURL;

  if (aURL.startsWith(iiopURLcontext)) {
    Properties props = new Properties();
     props.put(javax.naming.Context.PROVIDER_URL,
iiopURLcontext);
     props.put(javax.naming.Context.INITIAL_CONTEXT_FACTORY,
         "com.ibm.jndi.CosNaming.CNInitialContextFactory");
    System.out.println("Utils: Getting initial context.");
    context = new javax.naming.InitialContext(props);

    lookupName = aURL.substring(iiopURLcontext.length());

  } else {
       System.out.println("Utils: Getting initial default
context.");
    context = new javax.naming.InitialContext();
  }
  System.out.println("Utils: got initial context. Looking up:
"+lookupName);
  result = context.lookup(lookupName);
  return result;
}
```

Creating the Customer Client Bean

1. Create a new package called `com.ibm.ejbatwork.clients` (as detailed in "Create the Product Entity Bean" on page 167).

2. Select this package, then click on the right mouse button and select **Add -> Class**.

3. Type `CustomerClient` for the Class Name. and ensure that the **Compose the Class Visually** is checked. Click on **Finish**.

4. Select the other tool category by clicking on the **Swing** pull-down and selecting **Other**.

5. Select the **Variable tool** [ ] and drop a variable on the white work area by clicking on the left mouse button.

6. Click on the right mouse button and select **Change Type**. Select **CustomerClient**. Then, click on the **OK** button.

7. Change the Bean name to `CustomerClient` by clicking on the right mouse button and selecting **Change Bean Name**. Click on **OK**.

8. Select the **Bean Info** tab.

9. Three indexed properties need to be defined for the Bean: `Int[] prodNum`, `double[] price`, and `String[] prodName`. Use the following process for each of these:

   a. Click on the right mouse button and select **New Property Feature**.

   b. Enter the name and type for each property. Ensure that only **Readable** and **Indexed** are checked.

   c. Click on **Finish**.

10. Close the **CustomerClient** window and click on **Yes** to save the changes. VisualAge now generates the code; two get methods are defined for each property.

11. Add the following instance variables to the `CustomerClient` class:
    ```
    private CustomerSession customerSession;
    private Product[] products;
    ```

12. Open the `initialize()` method for CustomerClient and add the following code to the body.
    ```
    CustomerSessionHome customerSessionHome = null;
    javax.naming.InitialContext initContext = null;

    try {
        System.out.println("Retrieving initial context...");
        java.util.Hashtable properties = new java.util.Hashtable(2);
        properties.put(javax.naming.Context.PROVIDER_URL, "iiop:///");
        properties.put(javax.naming.Context.INITIAL_CONTEXT_FACTORY,
          "com.ibm.jndi.CosNaming.CNInitialContextFactory");
        initContext = new javax.naming.InitialContext(properties);
    } catch (javax.naming.NamingException e) {
    ```

```
        System.out.println("Error retrieving the initial context: " +
e.getMessage());
        System.exit(0);
}

// lookup the home interface using the JNDI name
try {
    System.out.println("Retrieving the home interface...");
        java.lang.Object o = initContext.lookup("CustomerSession");
    // this is the JNDI name
        if (o instanceof org.omg.CORBA.Object)
                customerSessionHome =
            CustomerSessionHomeHelper.narrow((org.omg.CORBA.Object) o);
} catch (javax.naming.NamingException e) {
    System.out.println("Error retrieving the home interface: " +
e.getMessage());
    System.exit(0);
} // end try

// Create a new CustomerSession to return
System.out.println("Creating new CustomerSession...");
CustomerSession customerSession = null;
try {
    customerSession = customerSessionHome.create();
        System.out.println("CustomerSession created!");
        Enumeration enum = customerSession.listAllProducts();
        Vector productVector=new Vector();
        while (enum.hasMoreElements())
        {   productVector.addElement(enum.nextElement());}
        fieldNumberOfProducts = productVector.size();
    products = new Product[fieldNumberOfProducts];
    productVector.copyInto(products);
} catch (Exception e) {
        System.out.println("Exception creating new
customerSessionWorld: "
    + e.getMessage());
        System.exit(0);}
```

Save these changes by clicking on the right mouse button and selecting **Save**.

13. Edit the three `get()` methods: `getProdName(int)`, `getProdNum(int)`, and `getPrice(int)` for the properties we defined earlier, so that they return `products[index].getProdName()`, `products[index].getProdNum()`, and `products[index].getPrice()`.

Loading the Sample Code from the CD-ROM

Two steps are required to import sample code from the CD.

1. Select **FILE -> Import**, then find the repository file. `Sample2-Client-Server.dat`, which is in `<cd drive Sample2 Directory>`. The sample code will now be in the repository.

2. In the Projects pane click on the right mouse button. Select **ADD -> Project**.

    Select **ADD a Project** from the repository and select the **EJBatWork Project Version 1.0**.

All the code should now be in the VAJ workbench. You can check that by expanding the `EJBatWork` project; it should show two packages: `com.ibm.ejbatwork.beans` and `com.ibm.ejbatwork.clients`. If you click on the **EJB** tab, there should be an EJBatWork EJB group. If you expand that group, there should be two Beans: `Product` and `CustomerSession`.

Creating the EJB-to-Database Mappings

Now that the code has either been written or imported, we need to map the Product EJB to a database. So, let's start by creating the DB2 database.

Create the DB2 Database

We have provided a DB2 script to create the database. The script creates the `EJBAWORK` database and the `PRODUCTBEANTBL` table.

1. Start a **DB2 Command** window.

2. Type:
    `db2 -tf <cd drive Sample2 Directory>\EJBatWorkSamp1.clp.`

3. Enter `EXIT` to close the window.

4. Check that the EJBAWOR1 database has been created, using the DB2 Control Center Administration tool.

    a. Start the **DB2 Control Center Administration** tool.

    b. Expand all levels until you see `EJBAWOR1` database. There will be a table called `PRODUCTBEANTBL`.

    c. Move the mouse to this table and click on the right mouse button.

    d. Select **Show Sample Contents**. This pane should list the four products stored in the database that we display later.

Map the Product Bean to the DB2 Database

1. Go to the **EJB** tab.

2. Expand **EJBatWork Project**.

3. Click the right mouse button on **Product -> Open to -> Database Schema**.

4. Select the **Schemas** Menu item on the Schema Browser.

5. Select **Import/Export** schema.

6. Import **Schema** from database.

    a. The schema name is `ProductBeanTbl`.

    b. The connection type is `COM.ibm.db2.jdbc.app.DB2Driver`.

    c. The data source is `jdbc:db2:EJBAWORK`.

7. Click on **OK**.

8. Select **EJB Qualifier** and select **Build Table List**.

9. Select the `EJB PRODUCTBEANTBL` under the Tables pane.

10. Click **OK**. The schema browser shown in Figure 10–17 is displayed.

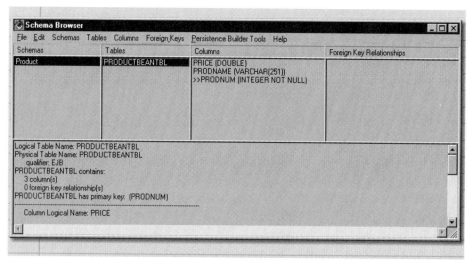

Figure 10–17 *Schema Browser Window*

11. Select **Schemas -> Generate Model** from Schema.

12. Close this window.

13. Click the right mouse button on **Product -> Open to -> Schema Maps**.

14. Select **Datastore Maps -> New EJB Group Map**. Type the following:
    Name: `ProductBeanTbl`
    EJB Group: `EJBatWork`
    Schema: `Select ProductBeanTbl`

15. Click **OK**.

16. Click on **ProductBeanTbl** (DataStoreMap).

17. Click on **Product**.

18. Select **Table Maps -> New Table Map -> Add Cluster Map no inheritance**.

19. Select **PRODUCTBEANTBL** and click **OK**.

20. Click on **PRODUCTBEANTBL** (in table maps column). The Map Browser shown in Figure 10–18 is displayed.

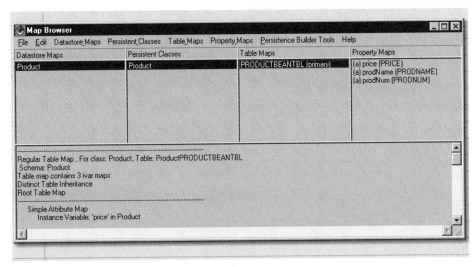

Figure 10–18 *Map Browser Window*

21. Click the right mouse button and click **Edit Property Maps**.

22. Map the class attributes to the equivalent table column with map type `simple`. Click on each cell to drop down a box; select options, as shown in Figure 10–19 (arrow 24).

23. Click **OK** (arrow 25 in Figure 10–19).

24. Close **Schema Browser**.

The fields of the `Product` Bean are now mapped to the columns of the PRODUCTBEANTL table in the EJBAWORK database.

We are now ready to test the code we have just developed, then to deploy the code into WebSphere.

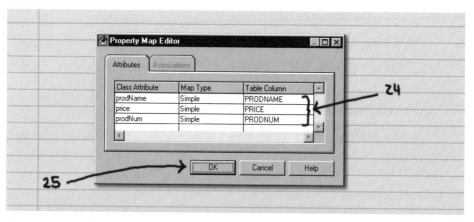

Figure 10–19 *Property Map Editor*

Testing the Beans Within VAJ

First we will test the `Product` EJB. VAJ provides a facility to automatically generate a test client. We will use that to generate a test client for the `Product` EJB, then one to test the `CustomerSession` EJB. Finally we will test the code end-to-end using the Java Server Page.

Test the Product Bean

1.   Go to the **EJB** tab.

2.   Expand the **EJBatWork Project**.

3.   Select **Product** and click the right mouse button to select **Generate -> Test Client**.

4.   Select the **EJBatWork EJB Group**.

5.   Click the right mouse button on **Add to -> Server Configuration**.

6.   Select **EJB Server**.

7.   Click right mouse button on **Properties**.

8.   Change the **Database URL** to **jdbc:db2:EJBAWORK** and click **OK**.

9.   Start the **Location Service Daemon** (click right mouse button and **Start Server**). The console appears, showing that the daemon has started.

10. Start **Persistent Name Server** (click right mouse button and **Start Server**). The PNS should show on the console.

11. Start the **EJB Server** (Click right mouse button and **Start Server**). The **EJS** will show on the console.

12. Click on **EJS** in the console to view the messages as the server starts. Lots of Debug messages will appear on the EJB console as it starts and loads the server and containers and completes the initialization steps.

13. Wait for the following message to appear on the EJS console.

```
{Product=com.ibm.ejbatwork.beans._ProductHomeSkeleton@...
CustomerSession=com.ibm.ejbatwork.beans._CustomerSession
HomeSkeleton@...}
```

This message indicates that the EJS server is ready to accept messages.

14. Return to the **VAJ Workbench**.

15. Select **Product**.

16. Click the right mouse button on **Run Test Client.** The **Test Client** window appears.

17. Resize the windows so that the **Console** and **Product Test Client** windows are both visible. Then, click on the **Connect** button in the test client window. A number of messages appear on the EJS console as the test client finds the home interface. Once the `Product` EJB is connected, its remote methods are visible in the Test Client window.

18. Select **findAllProducts() -->** Click **Send** (in test client window). The console will show progress as the methods are processed. Once this step is completed, the remote Interface appears on the Test Client window. There should be four remote objects in the drop-down box. These are the result of the `findAllProducts()` method.

19. Select the **getProdName()** method to view the product name for the remote object. The result in the Test Client window shows the product name. At this stage you might like to explore the facilities of the test client so that you can understand the range of facilities it provides.

20. Close the **Product Test Client** and return to the Workbench.

Test the CustomerSession EJB

1. Generate the test client for `CustomerSession` EJB as for `Product` EJB above.

2. Run the test client.

3. Invoke the `create()` method for this `CustomerSession` to create a `CustomerSession` instance.

4. Invoke the `listAllProducts()` method to list all the products in the database. An enumeration of the products is returned.

Execute the JSP, Using VAJ

VAJ provides a test environment for JSP, using its internal Web server. The steps below explain how to start the server and how to run the JSP. The JSP can be found in the WebPages directory on the accompanying CD.

1. Make sure the IBM WebSphere Test Environment feature has been loaded into your VAJ project workspace. This can be accomplished by checking the Workbench Projects page. You should see a project for IBM WebSphere Test Environment. If this project doesn't appear in the Projects page, complete the following actions.

    a. In the Workbench Projects page, select **File -> Quick Start-> Add Features**. The Quick Start dialog appears.

    b. Click **OK**. The Selection Required dialog box pops up.

    c. Select the **IBM WebSphere Test Environment** feature from the list of available features.

    d. Click **OK**.

2. Launch the WebSphere Application Server. To run the SERunner class, use the left mouse button to select the **IBM WebSphere Test Environment.** Next, click the selection with the right mouse button. A drop-down menu appears.

3. From the drop-down menu, select **Run -> Run main...**

Once the Web server has started, wait for two `Port 80:...` messages to appear on the console for the Web server.

Then, copy the `CustomerProduct.jsp` page located on the CD-ROM in the WebPages directory to the HTML directory that you chose during installation of the test environment. Start a browser and open URL `http://localhost:8080/CustomerProduct.jsp`.

A page like that shown in Figure 10–20 appears.

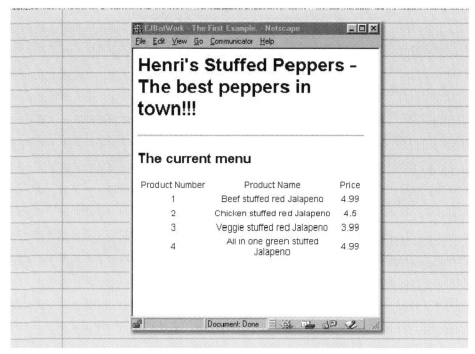

Figure 10–20   *Result from the CustomerProducts JSP*

Deploy the Code to WebSphere

Now that we have tested the code within VAJ, we need to deploy it to WebSphere. During the next set of steps, we create two Jar files: one for the EJBs and one for the client. Then, we define the containers for WebSphere to load the Jar Beans. Finally, we open the JSP in a browser to show the code end-to-end.

1. Create the EJS Jar files.

    a. Go to **EJB** tab.

    b. Select **EJBatWork Project.** Press the right mouse button, then select **Generate -> Deployed code**.

    c. Select **OK** to create an open edition.

    d. With the mouse at the EJBatWork project, click the right mouse button in EJB and select **Export -> EJS Jar.**

    e. Save the **EJS Jar file** as EJBatWorkSvrSmp1.jar

    f. Ensure that two Beans, `Product` and `CustomerSession` have been selected. (**Important:** The **Utils class** must be selected. When you are done, there will be a total of 32 class files.)

    g. Click on **Finish**.

2.   Create the Client Jar file.

    a. Select the **Projects** tab.

    b. Expand **EJBatWork Project**.

    c. Select the **com.ibm.ejbatwork.client** package.

    d. Click the right mouse button on **Export -> Jar file**. Select all the class files with **_Customer, CustomerSessionHome**, and all those by default. You should have selected a total of eight classes.

    e. Save this selection as `EJBatWorkCliSmp1.jar`.

    f. Select **Finish** to create the Jar file.

3.   Set up Lotus Domino Go and WebSphere + EJS as detailed in "Installation of IBM WebSphere and Enterprise Java Server" on page 207. Once they have been installed, update properties files as follows:

    a. Enable the WebSphere console by changing

```
debug.server.console.enabled=false
```

to

```
debug.server.console.enabled=true
```

in the `debug.properties` file in the `<WebSphere>\properties\server\servlet` directory.

    b. Set naming service to point to the **default JNDI port - 900** by changing the following three lines:

```
ports.lowerbound=9010
ports.upperbound=9030
ports.bootstrap=9020
```

to

```
ports.lowerbound=890
ports.upperbound=910
ports.bootstrap=900
```

in the `controller.properties` file in the `<WebSphere>\properties\server\servlet` directory.

    c. Update the **port 9020** in the `IBMNameServiceConfig.properties` file in the `<WebSphere>\propoerties\ejs` directory to **900** by changing

```
defaultNameServer=9020@localhost
```

to

```
defaultNameServer=900@localhost
```

4. Deploy the Jar files by copying them into `<WebSphere>\lib` directory. Since the EJS files from VisualAge are already customized for EJS, they do not need to be changed. Also, WebSphere will automatically load the files in its `lib` directory into the `CLASSPATH` at startup time, so we do not need to explicitly define the path. Alternatively, the Jar file loading can be specifically defined, using the instructions in the *EJS Quick Beginnings Guide*.

5. Define the containers for the EJS.

   a. Rename the current `ejs.properties` file in `C:\WebSphere\AppServer\Properties\ejs` to `ejs.properties.original` or another unique name. **Note:** Ensure that the file type is not `properties`; otherwise, it will be loaded.

   b. Copy the `ejs.properties.ejbatwork1` file to `C:\WebSphere\AppServer\properties\ejs`

   c. Rename this file to `ejs.properties`. You might want to edit this file so you can view the container configuration. Two containers are defined: one for the `Product` Bean and one for the `CustomerSession` Bean. The database to be used for the `Product` Bean is also defined here.

6. Install the JSP files into the Lotus Domino Go HTML directory.

   a. Create a new folder—EJBatWork—in the `c:\WWW\HTML` directory.

   b. Copy the three files—`CustomerProjects.jsp`, `CustomerSessionColor.jsp`, and `HSPheader.gif`—to the `C:\WWW\HTML\EJBatWork` directory.

7. Start Lotus Domino Go (execute the `gHTTPd.exe` in `C:\WWW\BIN` directory). This step should start Lotus Domino Go, WebSphere, and Enterprise Java server. Two consoles appear: Lotus Domino Go and WebSphere. On the WebSphere Console—Trace Output tab—you will see three messages indicating that the server and the containers have been started.

8. Start a browser and open `http://localhost/EJBatWork/CustomerProducts.jsp`

   This step returns a page with all the products in the database.

9.   For a more colorful version, try:

   `http://localhost/EJBatWork/CustomerSessionColor.jsp`

Conclusion

This sample has shown you how to create both Entity and Session Beans, how to access these with a Java Bean, and how to view the fields of a Java Bean by using a JavaServer Page.

To create the system for Henri, there are still some problems, so we need to develop the rest of the functions.

Notes and Guidelines

To simplify the process of adapting the generated code to work with an existing DB2 table, follow these rules when creating your Entity Bean.

- Make sure that your Bean's remote interface has the same name as your existing DB2 table, changing the case of the letters if you want. For example, if you have an existing table called `EMPLOYEE`, you could make your Bean's remote interface class name something like `Employee`.

- Make the names of your Bean's container-managed fields the same as the names of the existing table columns they correspond to, again changing case if desired. For example, if the table has a column named `EMPNO`, you could name the corresponding public field in your Entity Bean something like `empNo`.

Sample 3 — Creating the Ordering System

This example shows the development and deployment of a Bean-managed Entity Bean, `Order`, and how to work with prefabricated EJBs. This sample also shows how JavaServer Pages can be used to input information to a database.

In our scenario, this sample allows a customer to view the product menu that is provided by Henri's Stuffed Peppers restaurant. It implements the `CustomerSession` and `Products` portion of the object model. In addition to allowing access to these EJBs from a browser, we develop a JSP and associated customer client Java Bean.

Henri's Ordering Overall System Structure

This section builds on the previous system created in "Sample 2 — Creating the Product and Customer Session EJBs" on page 163. Figure 10–21 illustrates the overall structure of the new system.

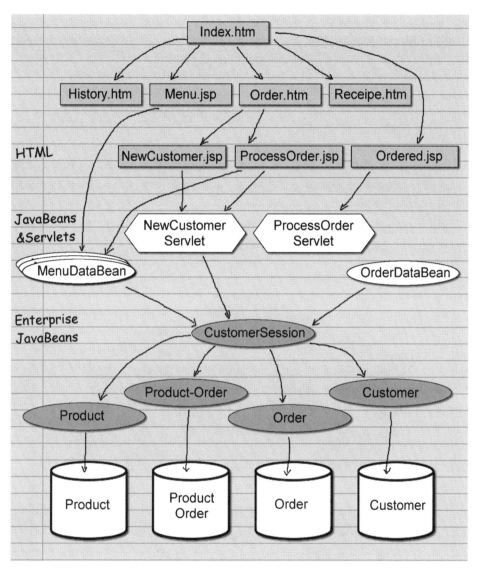

Figure 10–21 *Structure of Sample 3*

The top layer of Figure 10–21 shows the HTML and the JavaServer Pages for the site. In the next layer are the Java Beans and the servlets used to access the Enterprise Java Beans. The `CustomerSession` EJB is the focal point for access all the Entity EJBs. Finally, the Entity Beans access the database layer. The remainder of this section shows the HTML layer.

The HTML Layer of the System

Home Page — index.htm

The page shown in Figure 10–22 is the first page presented to Henri's customers. This page uses standard HTML facilities and can be used and accessed by any browser that supports HTML. The two links that are of interest are `The Menu` and `Order Stuffed Peppers`. Clicking on **The Menu** button loads the `Menu.JSP` page.

Figure 10–22 *Henri's Stuffed Peppers: Home Page (index.htm)*

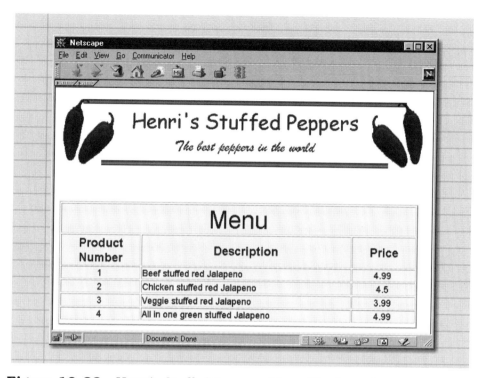

Figure 10-23 *Henri's Stuffed Peppers: Menu (CustomerSessionColor.jsp)*

Menu Page — menu.htm

menu.htm is the JSP page and associates the Beans that we developed in the previous section. Figure 10–23 shows a sample of the results from this page. Essentially, the JSP page uses the properties from the CustomerClient Java Bean. This Bean creates a new CustomerSession EJB, and then invokes its listAllProducts() method. This method uses the findAllProducts method of the Product EJB's home interface.

Order Page — order.htm

order.htm starts the process of ordering stuffed peppers. The first stage of the process is to identify the customer. Two options are presented to customers. The first is to enter their customer number if they are already registered as a customer. In this case, the page links to the ProcessOrder JSP. The second option is to enter their details and get a new customer number. In this case, the NewCustomer JSP

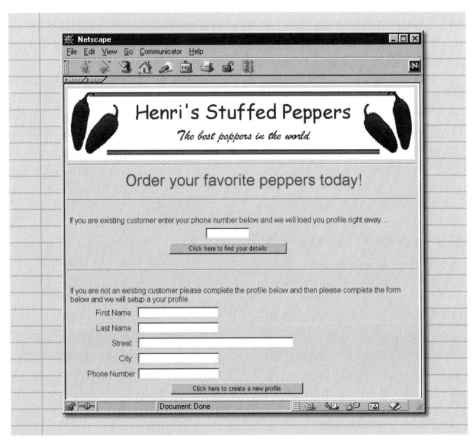

Figure 10–24 *Henri's Stuffed Peppers: Identify the Customer (Order.htm)*

and the associated `NewCustomer` Bean are instantiated with the data collected from the order HTML page. Figure 10–24 shows a sample of the page.

NewCustomer Page — NewCustomer.jsp

Once customers have entered their details in the order page and clicked on the Click Here to Create a New Profile button, this JSP page is loaded. The associated JavaBean `NewCustomer` is instantiated with the details from the order page. The Bean creates a new customer by using CustomerSession's `createCustomer` method. The JSP page displays the Customer Number that has been created, and the customer has to click on the button to return to the order page. There, the customer can enter the customer number and place an order. Figure 10–25 shows a sample of the output from this page.

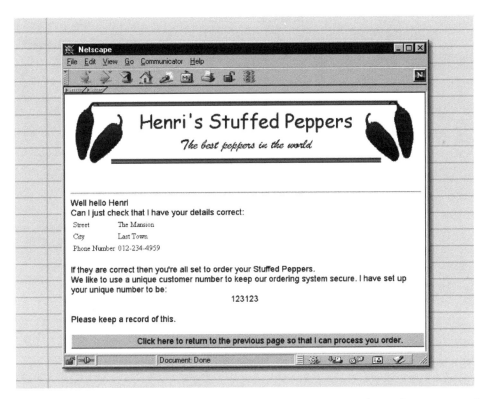

Figure 10–25 *Henri's Stuffed Peppers: NewCustomer (NewCustomer.jsp)*

ProcessOrder Page — ProcessOrder.jsp

This JavaServer Page is essentially an enhancement of the Menu JSP. The enhancement is to provide a column in the table for the customer to enter the quantity to be ordered. The quantity is stored in a multivalued property q to simplify the associated servlet, ProcessOrder. All the servlet has to do is to retrieve the array of values for the property and use that array to instantiate the HSPOrder Bean. The servlet is also responsible for calling the next page. Figure 10–26 shows a sample of the output from this page.

Ordered Page — ordered.jsp

The Ordered JavaServer Page is loaded by the ProcessOrder servlet. The servlet essentially creates an HSPOrder Bean, and the page displays the firstName and orderNumber properties of the HSPOrder Bean. From this page the customer can click on the button to return to the home page. Figure 10–27 shows a sample Ordered page.

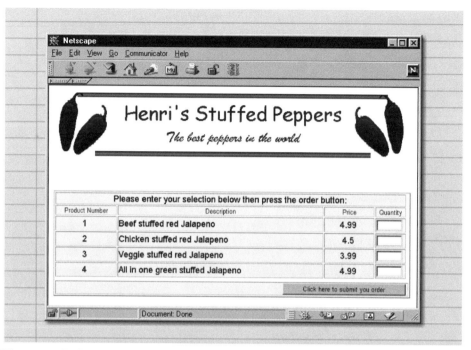

Figure 10–26 *Henri's Stuffed Peppers: ProcessOrder (ProcessOrder.jsp)*

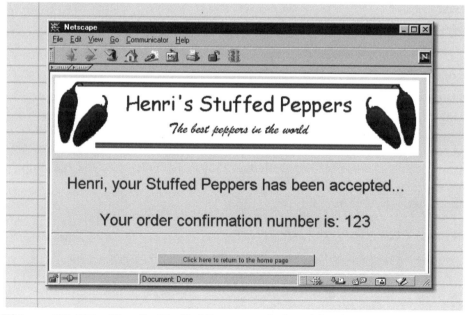

Figure 10–27 *Henri's Stuffed Peppers: Ordered (Ordered.jsp)*

System Notes

Restoring the System from the CD-ROM

The CD-ROM provided with this book contains the directory tree with all the files used in this book. The files are stored in two different ways: as a source and class tree and also as exports `*.dat` VisualAge for Java files. This storage allows you to simply browse the files in the CD-ROM or to include the `*.dat` files in your development environment.

Deploying the Jar Files and Setting Up the Web Pages

When using the application outside the VisualAge test Sandbox, the developer has to move the different files in the corresponding directories used by WebSphere. The servlets must be located in the `...\WebSphere\AppServer\Servlet` directory. The client and EJBs Beans and Jar files in the `...\WebSphere\lib` directory. The EJB `properties` file has to be set appropriately in the `...\WebSphere\AppServer\EJS`, then the `*.html` and `*.jsp` files have to be copied into `...\WebSphere\WWW\EJBatWork`.

Appendix A

Products

This appendix provides a brief, technical overview of all the products used for development, deployment, and execution of the sample EJB@Work Enterprise JavaBeans. Specifically, the appendix provides a description of the following products:

- WebSphere Application Server Version 2.0

- Lotus Domino Go WebServer Version 4.6.2.5

- DB2 UDB Version 5.x

- VisualAge for Java Version 2.1, Enterprise Edition

Note that these products are not included on the CD-ROM accompanying this book.

The appendix also describes the operating environment—the operating system requirements and the hardware requirements—that supports the EJB samples.

Introduction

To exercise the EJB@Work samples, you will use a number of different software products for the execution of both client- and server-side Web applications. Additionally, you will need certain products to support of the application development environment. Figure A–1 shows the overall runtime infrastructure.

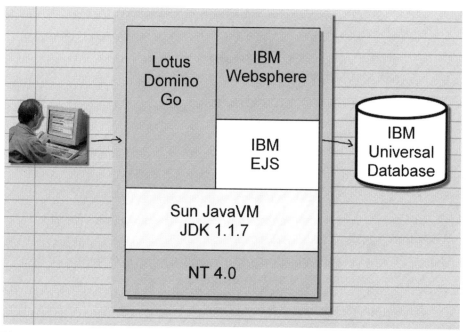

Figure A–1   *Infrastructure Required to Exercise the EJB@Work Samples*

We used the following server components during our tests:

- IBM WebSphere Application Server 2.0
- Lotus Domino Go WebServer 4.6.2.5
- IBM DB2 UDB Version 5.2
- Java Development Kit (JDK) 1.1.7

For the client environment we used:

- Web browsers:

- Netscape Communicator 4.0.5 (or later) with JDK 1.1.5
- Microsoft Internet Explorer 4

For the application development we used:

- IBM VisualAge for Java 2.1 Enterprise Edition

The operating system used for all the systems:

- Windows NT 4.0 with Service Pack 3.

WebSphere Application Server + IBM Enterprise Java Server

IBM WebSphere Application Server 2.0 is an implementation of the IBM Enterprise server for Java, which is based on the JavaSoft *Java for the Enterprise Initiative*. It is an evolution of what has been traditionally known as the Web server. The addition of the term *application* acknowledges the fact that this server not only serves HTML but now also serves industry-strength business applications. In some ways it is also the gateway to data and applications on back-end, three-tier systems. A large number of applications on the Web server are simply gateways to an existing back-end application or server and use a set of connectors for access to this back end. The three tiers of the WebSphere Application Server are the HTTP engine, the servlet engine, and the Enterprise JavaBeans engine (Enterprise Bean container). The server is designed to be open in order to work with general industry tools.

IBM VisualAge for Java Enterprise

IBM's VisualAge for Java Enterprise Edition is an award-winning Java application development environment for building Java applications, applets, servlets, and Java Beans components. Version 1.0 offered exceptional developer productivity, ease of use, and powerful features. Now, with a new High Performance compiler, connections to more enterprise systems, team programming support, and exploitation of the very latest in Java technology, VisualAge for Java Version 2.0 is simply the right choice for Java programmers.

VisualAge for Java Enterprise Edition provides all of the features of Professional Edition:

- Data Access Beans, so your Java application can access relational data from any JDBC-enabled database and make that data available on the Web
- Integrated development environment, including debugger and browsers
- Advanced visual composition editor

- Open Tools Integrator API

- Connection to VisualAge TeamConnection

- ClearCase and PVCS

- Enterprise Access Builder for CICS (ECI, EPI),

- TXSeries, SAP R/3, and CORBA

- Enterprise Java Bean tools creation and deployment

- Visual servlet builder

- Team programming for Java

- Enterprise toolkits for creating server-side solutions for AS/400 and S/390 High Performance compilers

- Remote debugger

IBM Universal Database

IBM's DB2 Universal Database is a relational database management system that is fully Web enabled and scalable from single processors to symmetric multiprocessors and to massively parallel clusters. DB2 UDB features multimedia capabilities with image, audio, video, text, and other advanced object relational support. With Version 5.2, DB2 UDB continues the evolution of advanced database technology begun in Version 5. It delivers more Web enablement with built-in Java support, client/server functions, more support for open industry standards, and improved performance and availability.

Expanded Data Type Support

DB2 Universal Database includes a number of new object relational data types for management of all of the data a business needs. With the new DATALINKS data type, files external to DB2 can be referenced and controlled by DB2. Coupled with the new DB2 file manager, AIX files now can be controlled with DB2's data integrity and intuitive user interface.

Data that is not in a relational format can be difficult for a database user to query. Now, with DB2's support of user-defined table functions, nonrelational data can be built in a tabular format that can be queried and captured in relational tables.

DB2 now delivers the DB2 Extenders to DB2 UDB EEE platforms—AIX, Windows NT, and Solaris. With EEE, the DB2 Extenders makes multimedia data support available to customers implementing clustered and parallel database configurations. This feature combines DB2's high-end scalability with its object-relational extensibility.

Online Analytical Processing (OLAP) and Optimization Features

DB2 now supports data storage on 4-Kbyte and 8-Kbyte pages. This support allows a single table or table partition to be up to 123 gigabytes—doubling the previous maximum.

New aggregation functions such as CUBE and ROLLUP allow the creation of supergroups for overall totals and cross-tabulations. The result is improved analytical processing performance.

Support for Java

IBM continues its support for industry standards and is the first database software provider to deliver SQLJ support, meaning greater usability and higher performance for Java database applications. Customers can use SQLJ as well as Perl, Java and JDBC, or Net.Data to access data from DB2 databases.

For Web application development, DB2 Universal Database also includes Java-based administration tools, VisualAge for Java, Net.Data, and the standard edition of IBM WebSphere Application Server.

Administering Databases over the Web

The DB2 Web Control Center now lets users perform administration tasks over the Web. In addition, DB2's comprehensive documentation can also be accessed from the Web.

Multimedia Object Support with DB2 Extenders

DB2 Universal Database provides integrated extenders for text, image, video, and audio objects. In addition, a wide variety of other extenders, including spatial, time series, currency, geographic information system (GIS), encryption, and optical, are available from IBM partners.

Improved System Monitoring Support for DB2 Connect

Certain commands have new parameters for collecting information on DB2 Connect applications. These new options return additional information about each user of DB2 Connect Enterprise Edition, including such important items as the current state of the user connection and the time that state was entered. In addition, new data elements have been added that monitor DB2 Connect application activity, allowing administrators an instant view of what each application user is doing.

Improved Scalability and Performance

DB2 now offers support for summary tables, removing the need for all queries to perform expensive, time-consuming joins in some application circumstances. Support for up to 125 terabytes of data is available.

Ease of Use

IBM offers new graphical tools on OS/2 and Windows 32-bit operating systems that make it easy to install, configure, and administer DB2 databases. From the Control Center, almost any administrative task can be accomplished. A number of Smart Guides walk customers through common tasks, such as configuring communications and creating tables. The graphical tools can also be used to administer any DB2 server on any of the available platforms.

From the Client Configuration Assistant, clients can configure communications to access remote or local DB2 servers.

Security Enhancements

Security additions include support for Open Software Foundation's Distributed Computing Environment (DCE). The DCE architecture is available to manage users, passwords, and groups more easily, and to authenticate users more securely. DB2 also provides a Trusted Clients option to choose whether to trust all clients or only those that come from an operating system with inherent security.

Additional Support for Communicating with Host Databases

Using DB2 Connect and the Distributed Relational Database Architecture (DRDA), DB2 Universal Database users can communicate with their host system. In addition to communicating with host systems using SNA, users can use TCP/IP to communicate with host systems that support this protocol. In addition, DB2 servers can accept requests from host systems using TCP/IP, allowing the use of a DB2 workstation server as an application server to a host application.

Appendix **B**

Installation of VisualAge for Java Enterprise

To produce Enterprise Java Beans and run or modify the samples provided on the CD-ROM, you must install and prepare VisualAge for Java (VAJ), as follows (note that VisualAge for Java is not included on the CD-ROM accompanying this book):

1. Install VisualAge for Java Enterprise 2.0

2. Install the VisualAge for Java Enterprise Update. The VAJ Enterprise Update contains code and documentation for the EJB Development Environment component and the JSP/Servlet Development Environment component to enable the use of the EJB Development Environment. If you are using a later version of VAJ 2.1 or VAJ 3.0, you will probably not need to update your VAJ.

3. Use the Enterprise JavaBeans Development Environment.

4. Add the **JDBC Driver** to the CLASSPATH environment variable.

5. Import the **IBM DB2 JDBC Drivers**.

6. Load the **samples** developed with VisualAge for Java.

Note: VisualAge for Java provides tutorials on how to get started with the VisualAge EJB Development Environment. You can access the tutorials by using the Help selection from the Menu Bar of any VisualAge for Java Window after the Enterprise Update has been installed:

```
Help -> Tools -> Enterprise Update
```

After you make the above selections, you will be presented with an HTML page for "VisualAge for Java Enterprise Update." From the HTML page, follow the hypertext link for SAMPLES to access the EJB Development Environment Samples and to take the tutorials.

Installing VisualAge for Java Enterprise 2.0

1. Run **Setup** from the supplied CD to install **VAJ 2.0**.

2. Restart your Windows NT machine.

3. Launch VAJ by clicking the **Start** button on the Windows NT taskbar. Then, select:

   Start **-> Programs -> IBM VisualAge for Java for Windows -> IBM VisualAge for Java**

4. **Exit** the VAJ Workbench by using the File dialog option.

5. Make a **backup** copy of the VAJ 2.0 workspace, saving the IDE.icx, ide.ini, and the repository ivj.dat files. The default installation procedure places these files as follows:
   ```
   <install-drive>:\IBMVJava\ide\PROGRAM\IDE.icx
   <install-drive>:\IBMVJava\ide\PROGRAM\ide.ini
   <install-drive>: \IBMVJava\ide\repository\ivj.dat
   ```

Important: Before installing the VisualAge for Java Enterprise Update, reboot your system and start **VisualAge for Java** in order to complete the post-installation processing. If this action is not completed, the Enterprise Update will not install correctly.

Note: If you get an error message from your Web browser when selecting any of the Help menu entries in VisualAge, it is likely that the installation did not successfully update the proxy exceptions list. In this case, manually append `local-host` to the browsers proxy exception list.

Installing VisualAge for Java Enterprise Update

1. **Unzip** the VAJ Enterprise Update file into a temporary directory on your Windows NT machine. The update file is located on the supplied CD.

2. **Run** the setup program located in the temporary directory. Follow the instructions on the install screens and use the default options.

3. **Restart** your Windows NT machine.

4. Use the **Start** button on the Windows NT taskbar to start VisualAge for Java.

Setting Up the Enterprise JavaBeans Development Environment

To use the EJB Development Environment, you must first load the required features, add the **JDBC driver** to the `CLASSPATH` for VisualAge for Java, and import the **DB2 JDBC drivers**.

The required steps are described in detail in the VisualAge for Java EJB Development Environment document, which is provided in HTML format. You can use the Help selection from any VisualAge for Java Window:

```
Help -> Tools -> Enterprise Update
```

After you make the above selections, you will be presented with an HTML page for "VisualAge for Java Enterprise Update." Follow the hypertext links for **TASKS -> Using the EJB Development Environment** for detailed instructions and additional information.

Loading the Required Features

1. Start VisualAge for Java by clicking the **Start** button on the Windows NT taskbar.

2. In the Workbench Projects page, select **File -> Quick Start**. The Quick Start dialog is displayed.

3. In the left pane, select **Features**, then in the right pane, select **Add Feature** and click **OK**. The Selection Required dialog is displayed.

4. In the Selection Required dialog, select **IBM EJB Development Environment** and click **OK**. The IBM EJB Development Environment feature is loaded. This step may take (more than) a moment.

Adding the JDBC Driver to the Class Path

To run and test Entity Beans in VisualAge for Java, you must add a JDBC driver to the `CLASSPATH` environmental variable and import the drivers into the IDE.

To add the DB2 JDBC driver to the class path:

1. In the Workbench Projects page, select **Windows -> Options...** The Options dialog is displayed.

2. In the tree view, select **Resources**. The Resources page is displayed in the dialog.

3. Beside the Workspace class path field, click the **Edit...** button to open a class path dialog.

4. Click the **Add Jar/Zip...** button and navigate to the following directory:
   `<install-drive>:\SQLLIB\java\`

5. Select the JDBC driver file **db2java.zip** and click **Open**.

6. In the class path dialog, click **OK**.

Importing the DB2 JDBC Drivers

1. Position your mouse in the All Projects pane of the IDE Workbench and click the right mouse button. Select **Add**, then select **Project ...**; the Add Project dialog is displayed.

2. Make sure the radio button for Create a new project named: is checked, then type the name for a new project called `IBM DB2 JDBC drivers`. Click **Finished**.

3. In the All Projects pane, you'll see the `IBM DB2 JDBC Project` that you just created. Select the **IBM DB2 JDBC Project** and click the right mouse button to go to the Import dialog. Select the radio button for **Jar file**, then click **Next** to go to the Import from a jar/zip file dialog.

4. On the Import from a jar/zip file dialog, type the directory and name of the JDBC driver as follows:
   `<install-drive>:\SQLLIB\java\db2java.zip`

5. On the Import from a jar/zip file dialog, make sure you've selected the checkbox for **.class.** Click **Finish**.

6. Review the All Projects pane of the IDE Workbench. You will find a project called `IBM DB2 JDBC Drivers`, with the following packages:

- `COM.ibm.db2.app`
- `COM.ibm.db2.jdbc.app`
- `COM.ibm.db2.jdbc.net`

You have now performed all steps that are required for "Using the Enterprise JavaBeans Development Environment."

If you are unfamiliar with the VisualAge for Java development environment, you may wish to complete the tutorials for Enterprise JavaBeans. The tutorials introduce you to the development environment, which enables you to accomplish activities such as creating and editing EJBs. You can access the tutorials by using the Help selection from the menu bar of any VisualAge for Java Window after the Enterprise Update has been installed:

```
Help -> Tools -> Enterprise Update
```

After you make the above selections, you will be presented with an HTML page for "VisualAge for Java Enterprise Update." From the HTML page, follow the link for `SAMPLES` to access the EJB Development Environment Samples and to take the tutorials.

Setting Up the JSP/Servlet Development Environment

The JSP/Servlet Development Environment requires the installation of VisualAge for Java Enterprise Update. Installation instructions for the Enterprise Update are documented in "Installing VisualAge for Java Enterprise Update" on page 201.

To use the VisualAge for Java JavaServer Pages (JSP) and Servlet Development Environment with Enterprise JavaBeans, you must load the required features and start the Java Web server in VisualAge for Java. You need not configure DB2 to work with data-enabled samples unless you will be accessing DB2 directly from the JSP/Servlet Development Environment. The required steps are described in detail in the HTML documentation "Using the JSP/Servlet Development Environment." You can access the HTML documentation by using the Help selection from the menu bar of any VisualAge for Java window:

```
Help -> Tools -> Enterprise Update
```

After you make the above selections, you will be presented with an HTML page for "VisualAge for Java Enterprise Update." From the HTML page, follow the hypertext links for **TASKS -> Using the JSP/Servlet Development Environment** for detailed instructions and additional information.

Loading the Required Features

1. Start VisualAge for Java by clicking the **Start** button on the Windows NT taskbar.

2. In the Workbench Projects page, select **File -> Quick Start**. The Quick Start dialog is displayed.

3. In the left pane, select **Features**, then in the right pane, select **Add Feature** and click **OK**. The Selection Required dialog is displayed.

4. In the Selection Required dialog, select the **IBM JSP Execution Monitor**, then click **OK**. The IBM JSP Execution Monitor feature is loaded.

5. Stop and **restart** the VisualAge for Java environment to complete the process for loading the required features into the repository.

Starting the Java Web Server in VisualAge for Java

1. Check the Workbench Projects page to make sure the IBM WebSphere Test Environment feature has been loaded into your IDE Project workspace. You should see a project for **IBM WebSphere Test Environment**. If this project does not appear in the Projects page, then complete the following actions:

    a. In the Workbench Projects page, select **File -> Quick Start -> Add Features**. The Quick Start dialog is displayed.

    b. Click **OK**. The Selection Required dialog box pops up.

    c. Select the **IBM WebSphere Test Environment** feature from the list of available features.

    d. Click **OK**.

2. Launch the WebSphere Application Server. To run the SERunner class, use your left mouse button to select the IBM WebSphere Test Environment. Next, click the selection with your right mouse button. A drop-down menu is displayed.

3. From the drop-down menu, make the following selection:

    ```
    Run -> Run main...
    ```

    You should now see a dialog for Run Program.

4. Using the Run Program dialogue, type SERunner in the pattern field and make sure that **com.ibm.servlet** is highlighted in the Package Names pane of the dialog. Click **OK**.

   If you encounter a Warning dialog box advising that "The resource directory could not be determined for all of the referenced projects," ignore the warning and click **Yes** to indicate that you still want to run the program. You will know that the server is successfully launched when you see the message endpoint.main.port=80 printed twice to the Console window.

Once you have the WebSphere Application Server running in VisualAge for Java, you can serve JSP files and HTML files from the designated document root; the document root is where your Web resources, including HTML files and JSP files, are stored. The designated document root was determined during installation of VisualAge for Java. During the installation process you were prompted to indicate the document root on your system. Make sure that the document root directory exists and is valid. The default location is:

```
<install-drive>:\www\html
```

Note: If you want to validate or change the document root, you can access it in the doc.properties file. This file is located in the following subdirectory:

```
<install-drive>:\IBMVJava\ide\project_resources\IBM
  WebSphere Test Environment\properties\server\servlet\
  httpservice\
```

Loading the Samples Developed with VisualAge for Java from the CD

To modify our sample code provided on the CD using VisualAge, you must first import the samples into the VisualAge repository.

Appendix C

Installation of IBM WebSphere and Enterprise Java Server

This appendix provides an overview of installation and operation of the IBM WebSphere and Enterprise Java Server. (Note that WebSphere, Enterprise Java Server, and any other products mentioned are not included on the CD-ROM accompanying this book.) The appendix includes these sections:

- Installing IBM's Enterprise Java Server
- Starting the server
- Stopping the server
- Updating server configuration files
- Deploying Enterprise JavaBeans

Installing the IBM Enterprise Java Server

To install the Enterprise Java Server:

1. Install these prerequisites (see their accompanying documentation):

    - JDK 1.1.7
    - Swing
    - DB2

2. Install Domino Go without Java Servlet Support or Web Server Search Engine. Follow the instructions in *Quick Beginnings* 3.9.4, pages 3–12, to configure Domino Go.

3. Install EJS Web Server by running **IBMWebAS33** for the latest 33B level.

    a. Disable JIT by renaming `SYMCJIT.DLL` in the Java `bin` directory if you are using Sun's JDK.

    b. If you are going to use the EJS samples, update the `boot-strap.properties` file in `\WebSphere\AppServer\properties` directory to include the following:

        - JDBC driver — `c:\sqllib\java\db2java.zip`
        - The client runtime Jar file — `C:\WebSphere\AppServer\samples\ejs\jars\EJSClientRuntime.jar`
        - The samples EJS directory — `C:\WebSphere\AppServer\samples\ejs`

4. If you are going to use the supplied EJB Samples, edit the `setSamples-ClassPath.bat` file in `<Samples dir>\ejs\bin` to include the correct directory names.

5. Enable console and debugging by editing the `debug.properties` file in `WebSphere\AppServer\properties\server\servlet` and changing

    ```
    debug.server.console.enable = false
    ```
    to
    ```
    debug.server.console.enable = true
    ```

    and
    ```
    trace.traceAll.state = off
    ```
    to
    ```
    trace.traceAll.state = on
    ```

Starting the Server

Start the server by double-clicking on the **Domino Go** icon on the desktop or by executing **wHTTPg.exe** in **WWW\bin**.

Either method should start the Domino Go console. A few seconds later, the WebSphere Application Server Console is displayed, showing debug information. Every few seconds, press the **Clear** button to clear the messages; otherwise, the display will freeze and you will not see any more debug messages.

Check that the three EJS components are started in the EJS status tab on the WebSphere console.

You can also access this console remotely by connecting to `port 9527` on the server. The default user ID is `admin` and the default password is also `admin`.

Stopping the Server

Stop the server either by selecting **File -> Exit** from the Domino Go console or by closing this console. Either method should close all the associated threads. You should check in the task manager that no unexpected Java tasks are running. If there are such tasks, kill them. If they do not stop, you will need to restart the server.

Updating the Server Configuration Files

The main configuration files are the `properties` files in various directories in the `C:\WebSphere\AppServer\properties\ejs`.

The main file that needs updating is the `ejs.properties` file in the `C:\WebSphere\AppServer\properties\ejs` directory. **Caution here**: WebSphere seems to load all the properties files in that directory. Make sure there is only one file with the file type properties!

The `ejs.properties` file is the one that can be managed by the `admin` GUI, so that file is the one that should be maintained. The `ejs.properties` file contains the definition for the containers and the Jar files that are deployed in the containers and must be modified to deploy Jar files. The Jar files to be deployed need to have the EJS associated stubs and a deployment descriptor.

Deploying Jar Files

Figure C–1 shows the stages in deploying a Jar file.

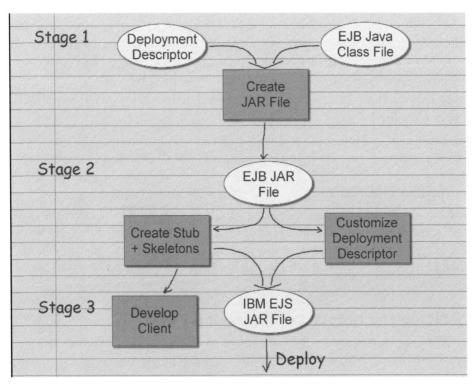

Figure C–1   *Stages in Deploying a Jar File*

There are essentially three stages. If you are using an EJS Jar file, then go to Stage 3. If you are deploying an EJB Jar file that includes a deployment descriptor, go to Stage 2. If you have a Jar file but need to create a deployment descriptor, go to step 2 in Stage 1. If you are starting from a set of class files, start at the beginning.

Stage 1: Creating the Jar File

1.   Create a Jar file if a set of class files have been provided. (The Jet tool should allow you to work with class files, but our use of the tool has been unsatisfactory.) Use the `jar cvf directory_name target_jar_file` to create the Jar file.

2.   If a deployment descriptor does not exist, then use the Jet tool to create one. (There is an icon for Jet on the desktop.) The `bat` file for Jet is in `c:\WebSphere\AppServer\samples\ejs\bin`.

a. Select the **source** Jar file name.

b. Use the **tabs** to define the deployment options.

c. Select the **target** Jar file name.

d. When finished, go to the **input/output** tab and click on **Build** to create the Jar file.

Stage 2: Creating an EJS Jar File

- Create an EJS Jar file by using the EJB deploy tool. We created a `bat` file for this purpose in the stand-alone directory `EJBDeploy`. The file takes two parameters: the source Jar file and the target Jar file.

Stage 3: Loading the EJS Jar File

1. Copy the Jar file into the `WebSphere\AppServer\lib` directory. Alternatively, you can copy the Jar files into another directory, which you must then add to the class path for EJS in the `bootstrap.properties` file and to the class path for the system.

2. Update the `ejs.properties` file to either create a new container for the Jar file or add the Jar file to an existing container.

3. Stop the server and restart it to cause the new `properties` file to take effect.

Running Clients

When you are running the client, the main thing to note is that `CLASSPATH` must include the directory that contains the `IBMNamingServer.properties` file. By default, this file is located in the `\WebSphere\AppServer\properties\ejs` directory. If you are running the client on a remote workstation, the `IBMNaming-Service.properties` file needs to point to the appropriate server. This information is detailed in *Quick Beginnings, Appendix A.*

The client needs access to a number of the EJS Jar files, so the appropriate class path definitions must be included. For convenience, we use the `Samples Classpath bat` file that we created.

Important Notes Regarding IBM EJS Deployment Tool

- Extra steps are required in order to use JDK collection classes (vector and enumeration). JCompile *must* be used to compile all of these classes, as documented in the IBM EJS Guide.

- The deployment tools support only top-down mapping of container-managed persistence EJBs to relational tables and does not offer options for this mapping.

- No configuration management capability is supplied by the deployment tool, which is file-based, so there is no special support beyond that provided by the WebSphere systems management utilities for repetitive, iterative cycles of import, deployment descriptor specification, and output of deployment code-generated Jar files. See the WebSphere systems management documentation for a description of scenarios and capabilities in this area.

- The remote interface name of a container-managed Entity Bean must not exceed 11 characters for DB2, as detailed in the *IBM EJS Integrators Quick Beginnings Guide.*

- The deployment tool handles all Beans. This handling includes generating EJB home implementations, `EJBObject` implementations, persister and finder implementations, and also generating stub and skeleton classes for the `RMI-over-IIOP`.

- The deployment tool handles only container-managed fields of primitive types.

- The deployment tool outputs a single Jar file that contains all the classes and interfaces for the EJBs. There is no partitioning of the Jar file into client- and server-oriented Jar files.

List of Abbreviations

APA   All Points Addressable

ACID   Atomicity, Consistency, Isolation, Durability

API   Application Programming Interface

CB_Connector   Component Broker Connector

CGI   Common Gateway Interface

CICS   Customer Information Control System

CORBA   Common Object Request Broker Architecture

DB2   IBM Database 2

DCE Distributed Computing Environment

DCOM   Distributed Component Object Model

DNA   Distributed InterNet Architecture (Microsoft)

DNS   Domain Name Service

DOM Design Object Model

DRDA Distributed Relational Database Architecture

DTP Distributed Transaction Processing (model)

EJB   Enterprise JavaBeans

ESJ Enterprise Server for Java

GUI Graphical User Interface

HTML Hypertext Markup Language

HTTP Hypertext Transfer Protocol

HTTPS Secure HTTP

IBM International Business Machines Corporation

IDL Interface Language Definition

IIOP Internet Inter-ORB Protocol

IMS Information Management System

IT Information Technology

ITSO International Technical Support Organization

JAR Java Archive

JCA Java Cryptography Architecture

JCE Java Cryptography Extension

JDBC Java Database Connectivity

JDK Java Development Kit

JIDL Java Interface Definition Language

JIT Just in Time

JMS Java Message Service

JNDI Java Naming and Directory Interface

JRMP Java Remote Message Protocol

JSDK Java Servlet Development Kit

JSP JavaServer Pages

JSQL Java SQL

JTA Java Transaction API

JTS Java Transaction Service

LDAP Lightweight Directory Access Protocol

MQSeries Message Queuing Series

NCSA National Center for Supercomputing Applications

NDS Netware Directory Services

NIS (YP) Network Information Service

NSAPI Netscape Server API

ODBC Open Database Connectivity (Microsoft)

OID Object Interaction Diagram

OMG Object Management Group

ORB Object Request Broker

OSI Open Systems Interconnection

OTS Object Transaction Service

RM Resource Manager

RMI Remote Method Invocation

RPC Remote Procedure Call

SNA Systems Network Architecture

SQL Structured Query Language

SSI Server Side Includes

SSL Secure Socket Layer

TM Transaction Manager

TP Transaction Processing

UDB Universal Database

URL Uniform Resource Locator

VAJ VisualAge for Java

VM Virtual Machine

WAS WebSphere Application Server

WWW World Wide Web

Index

http://www.phptr.com/

What's New? | What's Cool? | Destinations | Net Search | People | Software

PRENTICE HALL

Professional Technical Reference
Tomorrow's Solutions for Today's Professionals.

Keep Up-to-Date with

PH PTR Online!

We strive to stay on the cutting-edge of what's happening in professional computer science and engineering. Here's a bit of what you'll find when you stop by **www.phptr.com**:

@ Special interest areas offering our latest books, book series, software, features of the month, related links and other useful information to help you get the job done.

Deals, deals, deals! Come to our promotions section for the latest bargains offered to you exclusively from our retailers.

$ Need to find a bookstore? Chances are, there's a bookseller near you that carries a broad selection of PTR titles. Locate a Magnet bookstore near you at www.phptr.com.

! What's New at PH PTR? We don't just publish books for the professional community, we're a part of it. Check out our convention schedule, join an author chat, get the latest reviews and press releases on topics of interest to you.

Subscribe Today! **Join PH PTR's monthly email newsletter!**

Want to be kept up-to-date on your area of interest? Choose a targeted category on our website, and we'll keep you informed of the latest PH PTR products, author events, reviews and conferences in your interest area.

Visit our mailroom to subscribe today! **http://www.phptr.com/mail_lists**

LICENSE AGREEMENT AND LIMITED WARRANTY

READ THE FOLLOWING TERMS AND CONDITIONS CAREFULLY BEFORE OPENING THIS CD PACKAGE. THIS LEGAL DOCUMENT IS AN AGREEMENT BETWEEN YOU AND PRENTICE-HALL, INC. (THE "COMPANY"). BY OPENING THIS SEALED CD PACKAGE, YOU ARE AGREEING TO BE BOUND BY THESE TERMS AND CONDITIONS. IF YOU DO NOT AGREE WITH THESE TERMS AND CONDITIONS, DO NOT OPEN THE CD PACKAGE. PROMPTLY RETURN THE UNOPENED CD PACKAGE AND ALL ACCOMPANYING ITEMS TO THE PLACE YOU OBTAINED THEM FOR A FULL REFUND OF ANY SUMS YOU HAVE PAID.

1.   **GRANT OF LICENSE:** In consideration of your purchase of this book, and your agreement to abide by the terms and conditions of this Agreement, the Company grants to you a nonexclusive right to use and display the copy of the enclosed software program (hereinafter the "SOFTWARE") on a single computer (i.e., with a single CPU) at a single location so long as you comply with the terms of this Agreement. The Company reserves all rights not expressly granted to you under this Agreement.

2.   **OWNERSHIP OF SOFTWARE:** You own only the magnetic or physical media (the enclosed CD) on which the SOFTWARE is recorded or fixed, but the Company and the software developers retain all the rights, title, and ownership to the SOFTWARE recorded on the original CD copy(ies) and all subsequent copies of the SOFTWARE, regardless of the form or media on which the original or other copies may exist. This license is not a sale of the original SOFTWARE or any copy to you.

3.   **COPY RESTRICTIONS:** This SOFTWARE and the accompanying printed materials and user manual (the "Documentation") are the subject of copyright. The individual programs on the CD are copyrighted by the authors of each program. Some of the programs on the CD include separate licensing agreements. If you intend to use one of these programs, you must read and follow its accompanying license agreement. You may not copy the Documentation or the SOFTWARE, except that you may make a single copy of the SOFTWARE for backup or archival purposes only. You may be held legally responsible for any copying or copyright infringement which is caused or encouraged by your failure to abide by the terms of this restriction.

4.   **USE RESTRICTIONS:** You may not network the SOFTWARE or otherwise use it on more than one computer or computer terminal at the same time. You may physically transfer the SOFT-WARE from one computer to another provided that the SOFTWARE is used on only one computer at a time. You may not distribute copies of the SOFTWARE or Documentation to others. You may not reverse engineer, disassemble, decompile, modify, adapt, translate, or create derivative works based on the SOFTWARE or the Documentation without the prior written consent of the Company.

5.   **TRANSFER RESTRICTIONS:** The enclosed SOFTWARE is licensed only to you and may not be transferred to any one else without the prior written consent of the Company. Any unauthorized transfer of the SOFTWARE shall result in the immediate termination of this Agreement.

6.   **TERMINATION:** This license is effective until terminated. This license will terminate automatically without notice from the Company and become null and void if you fail to comply with any provisions or limitations of this license. Upon termination, you shall destroy the Documentation and all copies of the SOFTWARE. All provisions of this Agreement as to warranties, limitation of liability, remedies or damages, and our ownership rights shall survive termination.

7.   **MISCELLANEOUS:** This Agreement shall be construed in accordance with the laws of the United States of America and the State of New York and shall benefit the Company, its affiliates, and assignees.

8.   **LIMITED WARRANTY AND DISCLAIMER OF WARRANTY:** The Company warrants that the SOFTWARE, when properly used in accordance with the Documentation, will operate in substantial conformity with the description of the SOFTWARE set forth in the Documentation. The Company does not warrant that the SOFTWARE will meet your requirements or that the operation

of the SOFTWARE will be uninterrupted or error-free. The Company warrants that the media on which the SOFTWARE is delivered shall be free from defects in materials and workmanship under normal use for a period of thirty (30) days from the date of your purchase. Your only remedy and the Company's only obligation under these limited warranties is, at the Company's option, return of the warranted item for a refund of any amounts paid by you or replacement of the item. Any replacement of SOFTWARE or media under the warranties shall not extend the original warranty period. The limited warranty set forth above shall not apply to any SOFTWARE which the Company determines in good faith has been subject to misuse, neglect, improper installation, repair, alteration, or damage by you. EXCEPT FOR THE EXPRESSED WARRANTIES SET FORTH ABOVE, THE COMPANY DISCLAIMS ALL WARRANTIES, EXPRESS OR IMPLIED, INCLUDING WITHOUT LIMITATION, THE IMPLIED WARRANTIES OF MERCHANTABILITY AND FITNESS FOR A PARTICULAR PURPOSE. EXCEPT FOR THE EXPRESS WARRANTY SET FORTH ABOVE, THE COMPANY DOES NOT WARRANT, GUARANTEE, OR MAKE ANY REPRESENTATION REGARDING THE USE OR THE RESULTS OF THE USE OF THE SOFTWARE IN TERMS OF ITS CORRECTNESS, ACCURACY, RELIABILITY, CURRENTNESS, OR OTHERWISE.

IN NO EVENT, SHALL THE COMPANY OR ITS EMPLOYEES, AGENTS, SUPPLIERS, OR CONTRACTORS BE LIABLE FOR ANY INCIDENTAL, INDIRECT, SPECIAL, OR CONSEQUENTIAL DAMAGES ARISING OUT OF OR IN CONNECTION WITH THE LICENSE GRANTED UNDER THIS AGREEMENT, OR FOR LOSS OF USE, LOSS OF DATA, LOSS OF INCOME OR PROFIT, OR OTHER LOSSES, SUSTAINED AS A RESULT OF INJURY TO ANY PERSON, OR LOSS OF OR DAMAGE TO PROPERTY, OR CLAIMS OF THIRD PARTIES, EVEN IF THE COMPANY OR AN AUTHORIZED REPRESENTATIVE OF THE COMPANY HAS BEEN ADVISED OF THE POSSIBILITY OF SUCH DAMAGES. IN NO EVENT SHALL LIABILITY OF THE COMPANY FOR DAMAGES WITH RESPECT TO THE SOFTWARE EXCEED THE AMOUNTS ACTUALLY PAID BY YOU, IF ANY, FOR THE SOFTWARE.

SOME JURISDICTIONS DO NOT ALLOW THE LIMITATION OF IMPLIED WARRANTIES OR LIABILITY FOR INCIDENTAL, INDIRECT, SPECIAL, OR CONSEQUENTIAL DAMAGES, SO THE ABOVE LIMITATIONS MAY NOT ALWAYS APPLY. THE WARRANTIES IN THIS AGREEMENT GIVE YOU SPECIFIC LEGAL RIGHTS AND YOU MAY ALSO HAVE OTHER RIGHTS WHICH VARY IN ACCORDANCE WITH LOCAL LAW.

ACKNOWLEDGMENT

YOU ACKNOWLEDGE THAT YOU HAVE READ THIS AGREEMENT, UNDERSTAND IT, AND AGREE TO BE BOUND BY ITS TERMS AND CONDITIONS. YOU ALSO AGREE THAT THIS AGREEMENT IS THE COMPLETE AND EXCLUSIVE STATEMENT OF THE AGREEMENT BETWEEN YOU AND THE COMPANY AND SUPERSEDES ALL PROPOSALS OR PRIOR AGREEMENTS, ORAL, OR WRITTEN, AND ANY OTHER COMMUNICATIONS BETWEEN YOU AND THE COMPANY OR ANY REPRESENTATIVE OF THE COMPANY RELATING TO THE SUBJECT MATTER OF THIS AGREEMENT.

Should you have any questions concerning this Agreement or if you wish to contact the Company for any reason, please contact in writing at the address below.

Robin Short

Prentice Hall PTR

One Lake Street

Upper Saddle River, New Jersey 07458

ABOUT THE CD-ROM

The CD-ROM included with this book contains the source code used herein. The source code is presented in Java-structured ASCII/Directory source code and in the *.dat IBM VisualAge for Java repository format file. The reader can then browse directly the files in the structured by packages directories. In order to take full benefit of the book, the reader will need to download from the IBM websites starting at http://www.ibm.com the IBM DB2 for NT or Windows 95 V 5.2 or higher, and the corresponding IBM WebSphere Application Server V 2.0 or higher. The IBM VisualAge for Java with EJB support will need to be installed too.

The CD-ROM is organized in a set of directories containing the samples in the /Sample1, /Sample2, and /Sample 3 directories. The DB2 scripts are located in the /DB2Scripts directory. The web relevant files used will be found in the /WebPages and /WebSphereProperties directories.

Technical Support

Prentice Hall does not offer technical support for this software. However, if there is a problem with the media, you may obtain a replacement copy by e-mailing us with your problem at:

disc_exchange@prenhall.com